The Future of Israeli-Turkish Relations

Shira Efron

For more information on this publication, visit www.rand.org/t/RR2445

Library of Congress Control Number: 2018947061

ISBN: 978-1-9774-0086-4

Cover: cil86/stock.adobe.com

Support RAND

Make a tax-deductible charitable contribution at
www.rand.org/giving/contribute

www.rand.org

Preface

Since their inception, Israel-Turkey relations have been characterized by ups and downs; they have been particularly sensitive to developments related to the Arab-Israeli conflict. Throughout the countries' seven-decade history of bilateral ties, Turkey has downgraded its diplomatic relations with Israel three times, most recently in 2011. In May 2018, Turkey expelled the Israeli ambassador after Israel Defense Forces killed dozens of Palestinians during violent clashes in the Gaza Strip; Israel followed suit and expelled the Turkish consul in Jerusalem. While Turkey and Israel normalized relations in 2016, and, in principle, they share important economic and geostrategic interests, developments since then indicate that the two countries remain deeply divided on central issues, most notably the status of Palestine and its people, Iraqi Kurdish independence, and the composition of a postwar Syria. Turkey's divisions with the United States and its Arab Sunni ally countries, with which Israel shares important objectives, have only compounded these differences. In addition, Israeli and Turkish leaders, mainly Benjamin Netanyahu and Recep Tayyip Erdoğan, deeply mistrust each other, making it hard to put differences aside and focus on shared objectives.

This report examines the nature of Israeli-Turkish relations, with a particular focus on the Israeli perspective, and assesses the prospects for ties in the short- and medium-term future. It should be of interest to policymakers, analysts, and academic researchers studying Israel, Turkey, and the broader Middle East.

RAND Ventures

The RAND Corporation is a research organization that develops solutions to public policy challenges to help make communities throughout the world safer and more secure, healthier and more prosperous. RAND is nonprofit, nonpartisan, and committed to the public interest.

RAND Ventures is a vehicle for investing in policy solutions. Philanthropic contributions support our ability to take the long view, tackle tough and often controversial topics, and share our findings in innovative and compelling ways. RAND's research findings and recommendations are based on data and evidence, and therefore do not necessarily reflect the policy preferences or interests of its clients, donors, or supporters.

Funding for this venture was provided by the generous contributions of the RAND Center for Middle East Public Policy (CMEPP) Advisory Board, and the research was conducted within CMEPP, part of International Programs at the RAND Corporation. CMEPP brings together analytic excellence and regional expertise from across the RAND Corporation to address the most critical political, social, and economic challenges facing the Middle East. Support for this project is also provided, in part, by the income earned on client-funded research and by other donors.

For more information about the RAND Center for Middle East Public Policy, visit www.rand.org/cmepp or contact the center director (contact information is provided on the webpage).

Contents

Summary

In May 2018, another diplomatic crisis ensued between Israel and Turkey after Israel Defense Forces (IDF) killed dozens of Palestinians and injured over 2,000 in violent protests in Gaza. Turkey expelled the Israeli ambassador, and Israel in turn expelled the Turkish consul in Jerusalem. This diplomatic rift was linked with the opening of the U.S. embassy in Jerusalem, which followed U.S. President Donald Trump's recognition of Jerusalem as Israel's capital in December 2017. The announcement shattered years of precedent set by the international community and escalated tensions between Israel and Turkey; Turkish President Recep Tayyip Erdoğan convened an emergency gathering of Muslim leaders in Istanbul and criticized Israel by calling it "a terrorist" and "child-murderer" state. Both in December 2017 and May 2018, Israeli politicians retaliated by rebuking Erdoğan. Prime Minister Benjamin Netanyahu fired back, saying that Erdoğan was responsible for the bombing of Kurdish villages and helped terrorists who killed innocent people, including in Gaza.

These developments illustrate the state of ties between Israel and Turkey 20 months after the two countries restored full diplomatic relations. While Erdoğan's threat to cut ties with Israel—made before the Jerusalem announcement in an attempt to deter the White House from recognition—may not materialize, it is clear that despite mutual interests, the fundamental political differences between the two countries are far from resolved. This report, which draws largely on Israeli and third-party views, shows that, although the 2016 reconciliation encouraged various stakeholders eager to resume the decades-old bilateral Israeli-Turkish collaboration, diplomatic and security cooperation is unlikely anytime soon.

Since they began in 1949, Israel-Turkey relations have been extremely sensitive to developments on the Arab-Israeli front. After over a decade of close economic, diplomatic, and military ties, bilateral relations soured in the mid-2000s. The second intifada, the rise to power of Erdoğan's *Adalet ve Kalkınma Partisi* (AKP, or Justice and Development Party), the 2006 Second Lebanon War, and clashes over Israel's Gaza policies all exacerbated tensions, culminating in a 2010–2016 rift between the countries.

The larger regional context brought Israel and Turkey back together in June 2016, despite tensions largely centered on the Israeli-Palestinian conflict. Incentives for the thawing of relations included strong economic interests, chief of which was an energy deal that could transform Israel into a gas exporter and bolster Turkey as a key gas portal for Europe. Other considerations included satisfying the United States, which pushed the parties to resolve their differences, hoping to enlist two longtime allies to advance mutual interests and stability. In addition, Turkey and Israel were both anxious about the implications of a victory by Bashar al-Assad and the potential for permanent Russian, Iranian, and Hezbollah presence in Syria. Further, despite disagreements, both countries sought to find ways to alleviate the humanitarian crisis in Gaza.

On multiple levels, the 2016 rapprochement has enabled closer Israeli-Turkish cooperation, mainly on economic issues. However, incentives for collaboration have dissipated since 2016, making Israeli-Turkish ties precarious. First, while, as of January 2018, the gas deal is still formally considered economically and technically viable, Israel is examining alternatives that are politically less risky, focusing on the EastMed pipeline being negotiated with Cyprus, Greece, and Italy. Turkey had sought to reduce its energy dependence on Russian gas, especially since the 2015 crisis between Ankara and Moscow over Turkey's downing of a Russian bomber that violated its airspace; however, Ankara and Moscow have mended fences and are advancing the TurkStream gas pipeline from Russia to Turkey and the Akkuyu nuclear power plant project in Turkey, which is being built and will be operated by the Russian state–owned Rosatom.

Moreover, although Turkey was until mid-2017 the tip of the spear in the battle to overthrow the Assad regime (and break a critical node of Iranian influence), the Astana process—a Russian-Turkish-Iranian initiative—suggests that Turkey might concede its anti-Assad demands in return for preventing an autonomous, contiguous Kurdish region along its border with Syria. Concern over Ankara's quid pro quo with Tehran is shared by key Sunni Arab countries, including Jordan, Egypt, Saudi Arabia, and the United Arab Emirates, with which Israel has reportedly developed strong backchannel cooperation. Another threat shared by these countries is the emotional and ideological links between the AKP and the Muslim Brotherhood and its affiliated parties, including Hamas, which Israel and other countries consider a terrorist movement. These links cause Israel, and other countries in the region, to view Erdoğan's approach to the Israeli-Palestinian conflict as destabilizing.

Israel and Turkey still share certain important interests, primarily economic, and Turkey's size and location as a militarily capable Sunni country make it suitable to help contain Iranian influence in the region in the long run. Nevertheless, Israel's view is that as long as Erdoğan is in charge, diplomatic relations will be kept at a low profile. Historically, separation of economic interests from political differences has been possible, but this task might be harder today given the deep mistrust and tensions between the two countries. The 2016 post-coup atmosphere in Turkey adds to a more suspicious mindset, constraining efforts to advance relations.

The United States has traditionally had strong geopolitical, security, and economic interests in ensuring continued collaboration between Israel and Turkey.

Recently, Turkey's interests have diverged from those of the United States in several areas, including Middle Eastern affairs as well as domestic issues, complicating Washington's ability to partner with Ankara. Uncertain future Israeli-Turkish ties could compound these difficulties, undermining efforts to advance U.S. goals in the region by limiting the scope for enlisting two traditional allies.

Acknowledgments

I thank my formal peer reviewers, Howard Shatz, senior economist at the RAND Corporation, and Gallia Lindenstrauss, Research Fellow at the Institute for National Security Studies in Israel and a visiting fellow at the Bipartisan Policy Center, for their helpful feedback. I also thank Stephen Flanagan and Dalia Dassa Kaye for reviewing earlier versions of this report. I am grateful for the help of many individuals who enhanced my understating of the complexities of Israeli-Turkish ties, especially Nimrod Goren, Amit Mor, Alon Liel, and Ghaith al-Omari. Finally, I also recognize the generous support of RAND's Center for Middle East Public Policy for publishing this report.

Abbreviations

AKP	*Adalet ve Kalkınma Partisi* (Justice and Development Party)
BCM	billion cubic meters
CMEPP	Center for Middle East Public Policy
IDF	Israel Defense Forces
İHH	İnsani Yardım Vakfı (Humanitarian Relief Foundation)
MFA	Ministry of Foreign Affairs
NATO	North Atlantic Treaty Organization
NSC	National Security Council
PA	Palestinian Authority
PKK	*Partiya Karkerên Kurdistanê* (Kurdistan Workers Party)
PLO	Palestine Liberation Organization
QIZ	Qualifying Industrial Zone
TIKA	Turkish International Cooperation and Development Agency
UAE	United Arab Emirates
UAV	unmanned aerial vehicle
UN	United Nations
YPG	*Yekîneyên Parastina Gel* (People's Protection Units)

CHAPTER ONE

Introduction

In May 2018, another diplomatic crisis ensued between Israel and Turkey, after Israel Defense Forces (IDF) killed dozens of Palestinians and injured over 2,000 in violent protests in Gaza. Turkey recalled its ambassador to Israel; Israel followed suit and expelled the Turkish consul in Jerusalem, who represents Turkey to the Palestinian Authority. The expulsions were accompanied with public humiliations of diplomatic staff on each side; the Israeli ambassador went through a security screening at the Istanbul airport as he left, while the Turkish chargé d'affaires in Tel Aviv was summoned to the Israeli Foreign Ministry, where he underwent a public security screening.[1]

Just five months earlier, on December 9, 2017, in a speech in the central Turkish city of Sivas, Turkish President Recep Tayyip Erdoğan criticized Israel harshly, saying that "Palestine is an innocent victim . . . . As for Israel, it is a terrorist state, yes, terrorist! We will not abandon Jerusalem to the mercy of a state that kills children."[2] The statement came just after U.S. President Donald Trump recognized Jerusalem as Israel's capital and vowed to move the U.S. embassy there. Erdoğan warned the U.S. Administration, saying that "Jerusalem is the red line of Muslims," and before the announcement even threatened to sever ties with Israel over such an act.[3] In response, Israeli Education Minister Naftali Bennett said, "Erdogan does not miss an opportunity to attack Israel. . . . It's better to have a united Jerusalem than Erdogan's sympathy."[4] Israeli Prime Minister Benjamin Netanyahu went further, saying that he was "not used to receiving lectures about morality from the leader who bombs Kurdish villagers in his native Turkey, who jails journalists, who helps Iran go around international sanctions, and who helps terrorists, including in Gaza, kill innocent people."[5]

---

[1] Michael Bachner and *Times of Israel* staff, "Turkey, Israel Humiliate Each Others' Envoys in Escalating Diplomatic Tiff," *Times of Israel*, May 16, 2018.

[2] "Erdogan: Israel a 'Terrorist State' That Kills Children," *Times of Israel*, December 10, 2017.

[3] Amberin Zaman, "Erdoğan Draws Red Line over U.S. Embassy's Move to Jerusalem," *Al-Monitor*, December 5, 2017.

[4] Zaman, 2017.

[5] Herb Keinon, "Netanyahu Says Israel Will Not Be Lectured to by the Likes of Erdoğan," *Jerusalem Post*, December 10, 2017.

The mutual expulsion of diplomatic envoys and the vituperative rhetoric illustrate the current state of political ties between Israel and Turkey, approximately one-and-a-half years after the two countries normalized ties. While the reconciliation encouraged various stakeholders eager to resume the decades-old bilateral Israeli-Turkish collaboration, it is clear that notwithstanding mutual interests, the fundamental political differences between the two countries are far from resolved. Even though Erdoğan's threat to cut ties may not materialize in the near future, the diplomatic rift between the two countries is ever present.[6]

This report provides a unique insight into current Israeli thinking on the status of economic and political bilateral ties 20 months after normalization. It draws on reviews of academic literature and open-source reporting from Israel, Turkey, Europe, and the United States and reflects over a dozen in-depth conversations with current and former Israeli government officials, scholars, and journalists. As many of Turkey's traditional allies try to deal with a changed Turkey, it is useful to learn more about how a key U.S. partner with exceptional knowledge of the region views Ankara.

As subsequent chapters show, Israeli-Turkish relations have for many years been multilayered, with economic, geostrategic, and diplomatic dimensions. In summer 2016, multiple incentives existed for reconciliation, including strong economic interests—chief of which was an energy deal that could transform Israel into a gas exporter and bolster Turkey as a key gas portal for Europe. Other considerations included satisfying the United States, which pushed the parties to resolve their differences, hoping that its two longtime allies could again work together to advance mutual interests and regional stability. In addition, Turkey and Israel were both anxious about the implications of Bashar Assad's imminent victory and the prospect of a permanent Russian, Iranian, and Hezbollah presence in Syria. Further, despite disagreements, both countries sought to find ways to alleviate the humanitarian crisis in Gaza.

However, the incentives that brought Turkey and Israel together in 2016 have for the most part dissipated, making bilateral ties especially shaky. First, while the gas deal is still theoretically considered economically and technically viable, Israel is examining alternatives that are politically less risky, focusing on the EastMed pipeline being negotiated with Cyprus, Greece, and Italy.[7] Turkey has long sought to reduce its energy dependence on Russian gas, especially since the 2015 crisis between Ankara and Moscow, which developed after Turkey downed a Russian bomber that violated its airspace. However, Ankara and Moscow have mended fences and, as of January 2018, are

---

[6]   Turkish Foreign Minister Mevlüt Çavuşoğlu said in an interview with an Israeli newspaper that there is no danger to relations between Turkey and Israel ("Turkish FM: No Danger to Israel-Turkey Relations," *Arutz Sheva*, January 7, 2018).

[7]   "Israel Expects Gas to Flow from East Mediterranean to Europe," Associated Press, December 5, 2017.

advancing the TurkStream gas pipeline from Russia to Turkey and the Akkuyu nuclear power plant in Turkey, which is being built with Russian support.[8]

Meanwhile, U.S.-Turkish ties have deteriorated since the July 2016 coup attempt in Turkey and reached a "crisis point" after Turkey arrested U.S. consulate staff in Istanbul in October 2017.[9] Deep divides between Washington and Ankara over both domestic and foreign policy issues make renewed U.S. pressure on either Israel or Turkey to resolve their differences unlikely.[10]

The lack of international checks on Israel's Turkey stance became clear when Netanyahu was the first world leader announcing support for an independent Kurdish state carved out of Iraq, an idea that Turkey deeply opposes, as do other countries—including the United States.[11] This is not the first time that Netanyahu and Israeli government officials have backed this idea, but doing so publicly only two weeks before the September 25 referendum slated in Iraqi Kurdistan and a few days before the United Nations (UN) General Assembly's annual meeting, knowing that the United States and other countries opposed it, generated conspiracy theories in Turkey accusing Israel of meddling in Kurdish affairs.[12]

Moreover, although Turkey was until recently seen as the tip of the spear in the battle to overthrow the Assad regime, and with it break a critical node of Iranian influence, the Astana process—a Russian-Turkish-Iranian initiative—suggests that Turkey might concede its anti-Iranian demands in return for preventing an autonomous and contiguous Kurdish region along its border with Syria. The concern over Ankara's quid pro quo with Tehran is shared by key Sunni Arab countries, including Jordan, Egypt, Saudi Arabia, and the United Arab Emirates (UAE), with whom Israel has reportedly developed strong backchannel cooperation.[13] Another threat shared by these countries is the emotional and ideological link between Erdoğan's party, the *Adalet ve Kalkınma Partisi* (AKP, or Justice and Development Party), and the Muslim Brotherhood and affiliated actors including Hamas and Qatar, which Israel and other countries consider a terrorist movement. For that reason, Erdoğan's approach to the Israeli-Palestinian conflict is seen in Israel, as well as in parts of the broader region, as controversial and

---

[8]   "Putin to Visit Turkey and Egypt Amid Anger over Trump's Jerusalem Move," *Radio Free Europe*, December 8, 2017.

[9]   Verdi Tzou, "Visas Resume Between U.S. and Turkey After Ankara's Promises," *Cipher Brief*, November 6, 2017.

[10]   Soner Cagaptay, "Turkey and U.S. Enter Most Important Crisis in Recent Memory," *Cipher Brief*, October 1, 2017.

[11]   Jeffrey Heller, "Israel Endorses Independent Kurdish State," Reuters, September 13, 2017.

[12]   Tom O'Connor, "Turkey Tries to Scare Voters with Warning About Jews Ahead of Kurdish Referendum," *Newsweek*, September 15, 2017.

[13]   Uzi Rabi and Chelsi Mueller, "The Gulf Arab States and Israel Since 1967: From 'No Negotiation' to Tacit Cooperation," *British Journal of Middle Eastern Studies*, Vol. 44, No. 4, 2017, pp. 576–592.

destabilizing. On top of all, Erdoğan's anti-Israel stance is interpreted by Israelis not only as politically motivated but also as reflecting anti-Semitic views.[14] Many Turkish Jews are emigrating to other countries,[15] adding to the Israeli sense that Turkey is no longer a reliable partner.

Organization of This Report

Chapters Two and Three of this report describe the history of Israeli-Turkish relations and the six-year reconciliation process. Chapter Four outlines the status of bilateral economic relations, focusing on trade, tourism, and energy. Chapter Five introduces the key standing political dimensions between Israel and Turkey—the Palestinian issue, Syria and Iran, Kurdish independence, and Israel's new ties with Greece and Cyprus.

Finally, Chapter Six concludes with an assessment of the prospects for improvement of Israeli-Turkish relations. The key takeaway is that, whereas renewed ties between Israel and Turkey have allowed for expansion of economic relations, a resumption of past cooperation between the two countries on sensitive diplomatic and security issues is unlikely in the near future. From Israel's perspective, although Israeli-Turkish cooperation remains intact for now, diplomatic relations will be kept at a low profile as long as Erdoğan is in charge—and while historically, separation of economic interests from political differences was possible, this task might be harder today given deep mistrust.

---

[14] Dror Zeevi, "Ha'Antishemiyut Ha'Akrait Shel Erdoğan," *Forum for Regional Thinking*, September 3, 2013; Efrat Elron, *Antisemitism and Anti-Zionism in Turkey: From Ottoman Rule to AKP,* London: Routledge, 2017, pp. 213–214.

[15] Zvika Klein, "Biglal Ha'Antishemiyut: Yahadut Turkia Mechapeset Miklat, *M'aariv*, March 21, 2015.

CHAPTER TWO

A History of Ups and Downs in Bilateral Relations

Turkey and Israel, two non-Arab Middle Eastern powers, have long been considered natural allies. For decades, they have collaborated at different levels to counter the influence of their shared regional enemies. Despite this longtime cooperation, their relationship was transformed into strategic partnership only in the 1990s. This chapter reviews the evolution of Israeli-Turkish bilateral ties from Israel's foundation in 1948 to 2011, including the series of crises in 2009–2011 that marked the end of the two countries' strategic alliance.

1948–1990: Limited, Covert Ties

Turkey was one of the first countries—and the first Muslim-majority country—to recognize the state of Israel, doing so in 1949.[1] It subsequently followed a more cautious approach and kept its engagement with Israel mostly secretive, fearing Arab backlash.[2] Turkey's sensitivity to Arab opinion became apparent in 1956; after Israel invaded Egypt's Sinai Peninsula as part of the Suez Operation, Turkey downgraded its diplomatic ties with Israel to the level of chargés d'affaires.[3]

In 1958, Israeli Prime Minister David Ben Gurion and Turkish Prime Minister Adnan Menderes met secretly to form the basis for their countries' partnership, agreeing on the "peripheral pact," which would involve intelligence sharing and mutual support to strengthen the countries' respective militaries.[4] After the Six-Day War in 1967, Turkey joined the Arab countries in calling Israel to withdraw from the lands it occupied in the war. However, Turkey refrained from referring to Israel as an "aggressor state," as the Arab countries did. Nevertheless, in 1979, Palestinian leader Yasser

---

[1]   Washington Institute for Near East Policy, "Timeline of Turkish-Israeli Relations, 1949–2006," 2006.

[2]   Ofra Bengio, *Turkish-Israeli Relationship: Changing Ties of the Middle Eastern Outsiders*, London: Palgrave Macmillan, 2004.

[3]   "Turkey-Israel Relations: A Timeline," *Haberler.com*, June 27, 2016.

[4]   Washington Institute for Near East Policy, 2006.

Arafat traveled to Ankara to open an office for the Palestine Liberation Organization (PLO), which was then considered a terrorist organization by Israel, the United States, and other countries.[5] In 1980, Turkey downgraded its diplomatic relations with Israel to a symbolic level, citing Israel's annexation of East Jerusalem, which the Palestinians and most UN member states consider occupied territory.[6] Throughout the 1980s, Turkey showed no intention of repairing relations. It was only after the Madrid peace process in 1991 that Turkey reengaged with Israel at the ambassadorial level, and it concurrently elevated its diplomatic ties with the Palestinian Authority (PA) to the same level.[7]

1990s: Marriage of Convenience Transforms into Strategic Ties

In the 1990s, capitalizing on the post–Cold War environment and regional developments, including the Madrid Peace conference, the first Gulf War, and the Oslo Process, ties between Turkey and Israel deepened quickly, transforming from primarily economic relations to a strong security partnership.[8] The basis for the strategic Turkish-Israeli alliance in the 1990s was a marriage of convenience for both sides, sustained partly by the mutual perception of Syria as a security threat. Turkey's issues with Syria included its refusal to recognize Turkey's 1939 annexation of Hatay Province;[9] its allowing the terrorist group Armenian Secret Army for the Liberation of Armenia to operate against Turkey from then–Syrian-controlled Lebanon;[10] and its provision of logistical support to the Kurdistan Workers' Party (*Partiya Karkerên Kurdistanê*, or PKK).[11]

Seeking to modernize its military to better address multiple security challenges, Turkey benefitted from Israeli willingness to supply otherwise unavailable weapons.

---

[5]   Washington Institute for Near East Policy, 2006.

[6]   Ufuk Ulutas, "Turkey-Israel: A Fluctuating Alliance," *SETA Policy Brief*, No. 42, January 2010.

[7]   Meliha Altunışık, "The Turkish-Israeli Rapprochement in the Post–Cold War Era," *Middle Eastern Studies*, Vol. 36, No. 2, 2000, pp. 172–191.

[8]   Oğuz Çelikkol, *Turkish-Israeli Relations: Crises and Cooperation*, Israel-Turkey Policy Dialogue Publication Series, Global Political Trends Center, Istanbul Kultur University, and Mitvim, November 2016; Mahmut Bali Aykan, "The Turkey-U.S.- Israel Triangle: Continuity, Change, and Implications for Turkey's Post–Cold War Middle East Policy," *Journal of South Asian and Middle Eastern Studies*, Vol. 22, No. 4, Summer 1999.

[9]   "Syria and Turkey—A History of a Complex Relationship," *EU News*, July 28, 2015; during the rapprochement between Turkey and Syria in 2010, Syria reportedly did change its stance, and the issue was practically solved in 2011 (Emma Lundgren Jörum, *Beyond Syria's Borders: A History of Territorial Disputes in the Middle East*, London: IB Tauris, 2014, p. 105).

[10] These operations stopped in the 1980s.

[11] Kilic Bugra Kanat, "Turkish-Israeli Reset: Business as Usual?" *Middle East Policy Council*, Vol. 20, No. 2, Summer 2013; "Syria and Turkey—A History of a Complex Relationship," 2015.

Israel, in turn, gained as Turkey became a lucrative market for its defense industry.[12] Simultaneously, tourism and trade grew between the nations, and Turkey was considered one of Israel's closest friends on multiple levels. After a massive earthquake hit Turkey in 1999, Israel quickly offered help that reportedly saved many Turkish lives and engendered good will in Turkey.[13] In January 2000, Israel and Turkey signed an agreement that allowed Israel to purchase water from Turkey, and in June of that year, the two countries signed a first memorandum of understanding for promoting scientific cooperation.[14] Overall, what began as marriage of convenience between Israel and Turkey in earlier decades was celebrated as a honeymoon from 1992 to 2000.

2000s: The End of the Israeli-Turkish Honeymoon

The outbreak of the second intifada in late 2000, and the images of Israel Defense Forces (IDF) soldiers suppressing violence by Palestinian youth, had a negative influence on Turkish public opinion toward Israel.[15] Still, substantial military and civilian cooperation was maintained in 2001, including a bilateral exercise from the Marmaris Aksaz Deniz naval base and combined exercises among Israel, Turkey, and the United States. In early 2002, despite harsh anti-Israeli statements by Turkish politicians, bilateral relations remained strong. On the military level, for example, Turkey signed a secret agreement with Israeli military industries in 2002 to upgrade 170 M-60A1 Turkish tanks. In August, the two countries signed an agreement estimated at $1 billion to import Turkish water from the Manavgat River to Israel.[16] Israel, however, withdrew from the deal, opting for desalination instead, in a move that upset Turkey.[17]

In hindsight, the AKP's election victory in November 2002 signaled a shift in the alliance, as then–Prime Minister Erdoğan became more vocal about his anti-Israel sentiment. Nevertheless, diplomatic ties were not strained until 2004. In March 2004, after Israel assassinated Hamas leader Sheikh Ahmed Yassin, Erdoğan denounced the killing as a "terrorist act" and said that Israel conducts "state terror" in Gaza.[18] Despite early signs of a diplomatic downturn, ties with Israel were sustained and mili-

---

[12] Kanat, 2015.

[13] Alon Liel, "Turkey and Israel: A Chronicle of Bilateral Relations," Israel-Turkey Policy Dialogue Publication Series, Global Political Trends Center, Istanbul Kultur University, and Mitvim, February 2017.

[14] Washington Institute for Near East Policy, 2006.

[15] Liel, 2017.

[16] Washington Institute for Near East Policy, 2006.

[17] Nelson Zalman, "Did Israel Sign a Deal with Turkey to Import Water?" *Arutz Sheva*, July 7, 2009; email exchange with a Turkey expert at an Israeli think tank, January 19, 2018.

[18] Jean-Christophe Peuch, "Turkey: Prime Minister's Criticism of Israel Does Not Mark Shift in Policy," *Radio Free Europe*, June 10, 2004.

tary cooperation remained, with high-level visits by heads of the Turkish Air Force and Naval Forces and by the IDF chief of staff. In 2005, Turkey's military bought three unmanned aerial vehicle (UAV) systems from Israel Aircraft Industries and the Israeli company Elbit Systems for $183 million, and the IDF agreed to supply Turkey with surveillance equipment to better protect its border with Iraq.[19]

Considering Israeli plans to withdraw from Gaza, Erdoğan even visited Israel in May 2005—his first and only visit—and invited then–Israeli Prime Minister Ariel Sharon to visit Ankara. In September, Turkey brokered the first public official talks between Israel and Pakistan, an effort that was seen as part of Turkey's overall pursuit of a regional mediator role. The continued multilevel Israeli-Turkish partnership demonstrated that while Erdoğan did not sympathize with Israel, he was pragmatic. Erdoğan and the AKP's efforts during that period to engage American Jewish organizations in Washington to help lobby on their behalf in Congress further illustrated that point.[20]

However, Hamas's victory in the Palestinian legislative elections in January 2006, and the subsequent meeting between Hamas leaders and Turkish government officials at AKP headquarters, upset the Israeli-Turkish balance. Escalation of violence in Gaza and the Second Lebanon War led to anti-Israel rhetoric and widespread protests in Turkish cities. Still, even during these times, Israeli-Turkish ties were sustained; in 2007–2008, Turkey officially mediated highly sensitive and secretive talks between Israel and Syria, which reportedly were on the verge of being fruitful.[21]

A watershed moment in Israeli-Turkish ties came in late December 2008. Only three days after then–Israeli Prime Minister Ehud Olmert visited Ankara to discuss Turkish mediation efforts with Syria, Israel launched operation Cast Lead in Gaza. The operation not only ended the Israeli-Syrian peace process but also transformed Israeli-Turkish relations. Erdoğan was not informed of Israel's plans and had strong emotional ties with Gaza and its leadership,[22] and he saw the operation as both a personal insult and a blow to Israeli-Turkish bilateral ties.[23] Erdoğan's government responded harshly. He openly stated that he had lost confidence in Olmert and no longer considered him a "partner for peace." Further, in a publicized speech, he condemned Israel and the international community for accepting Israel's behavior, saying in Hebrew "*lo tirtzach*" ("thou shall not kill").[24]

---

[19]   Washington Institute for Near East Policy, 2006.

[20]   İlker Aytürk, "The Coming of an Ice Age? Turkish–Israeli Relations Since 2002," *Turkish Studies*, Vol. 12, No. 4, 2011, pp. 675–687.

[21]   Aytürk, 2011.

[22]   Liel, 2017.

[23]   Selin Nasi, "Turkey-Israel Deal: A Key to Long-Term Reconciliation?" Israel Turkey Policy Dialogue Publication Series, Global Political Trends Center, Istanbul Kultur University, and Mitvim, January 2017.

[24]   As cited by Aytürk, 2011 (translated from original reporting in Turkish).

Shortly afterward then–Israeli President Shimon Peres and Erdoğan clashed publicly on stage at the World Economic Forum in Davos. Erdoğan told Peres, "When it comes to killing, you know well how to kill" and left the stage angrily.[25] Erdoğan's rebukes—his tone and word choices—were (and are still) seen in Israel as reflection of his anti-Semitic views.[26] The heated rhetoric influenced leaders on both sides. Israeli politicians threatened to recognize the Armenian genocide if Turkey continued to refer to Israel's actions in Gaza as genocide.[27]

In October 2009, after a few months of attempts on both sides to soothe the growing animosity, including a meeting of the Turkish and Israeli foreign ministers,[28] Erdoğan blocked Israel from participating in the Anatolian Eagle Military Exercises. The United States and Italy pulled out of the exercises in protest, leading to their cancelation,[29] but Erdoğan did not budge, choosing to stoke bilateral tensions and domestic outrage further with anti-Israel actions and harsh rhetoric. This sentiment trickled down to public opinion, and two television series (one on a public network and another on a private one) portrayed Israel and the Jewish religion extremely negatively.[30]

Israel did not settle for traditional diplomatic protest. Then–Deputy Foreign Minister Danny Ayalon publicly humiliated the Turkish ambassador Oğuz Çelikkol, whom he summoned to protest the TV series, by having him sit on a lower stool and saying to the press, "The main thing is that you see that he is seated low and that we are high . . . that there is one flag on the table (the Israeli flag) and that we are not smiling"[31] Despite a formal apology,[32] the "low chair" incident led to further deterioration of relations. When then–Defense Minister Ehud Barak went to Ankara to mend ties, neither then–President Gul nor Erdoğan were willing to see him, and he met only with then–Foreign Minister Davutoglu.[33]

The most infamous Turkish-Israeli confrontation, May 2010's *Mavi Marmara* incident, weakened the already frayed ties with a direct violent conflict, the first in the

---

[25] Katrin Bennhold, "Leaders of Turkey and Israel Clash at Davos Panel," *New York Times*, January 29, 2009.

[26] Dror Zeevi, "Ha'Antishemiyut Ha'Akrait Shel Erdoğan," *Forum for Regional Thinking*, September 3, 2013.

[27] Liel, 2017.

[28] Barak Ravid, "Livni, Turkish FM Hold Reconciliation Talks in Brussels," *Haaretz*, March 6, 2009.

[29] Julian Borger, "Turkey Confirms It Barred Israel from Military Exercise Because of Gaza War," *The Guardian*, October 12, 2009.

[30] In the series on Turkish public television, IDF soldiers were portrayed as monstrous murderers of Palestinians in the West Bank and Gaza. See Michael Weiss, "Turkish TV Depicts IDF as Bloodthirsty," *Tablet Magazine*, October 15, 2009. The other show, on a private channel, was described as anti-Semitic. See "Israel-Turkey Tensions High over TV Series," *CNN*, January 12, 2010.

[31] "Israel-Turkey Tensions High over TV Series," 2010.

[32] Barak Ravid, "Peres: Humiliation of Turkey Envoy Does Not Reflect Israel's Diplomacy," *Haaretz*, January 13, 2010.

[33] Sami Moubayed, "Israel and Turkey Are Drifting Apart," *Gulf News*, January 19, 2010.

60-year history of Israeli-Turkish relations. Purchased by a Turkish Islamic nongovernmental organization called İHH (İnsani Yardım Vakfım or Humanitarian Relief Foundation), the *Mavi Marmara* was the largest ship taking part in what participants called the Gaza Freedom Flotilla, the purpose of which was to break Israel's naval blockade on Gaza. After the *Mavi Marmara* did not heed Israeli navy warnings, IDF commandos raided it, leading to the death of ten Turkish activists (one of whom was a dual U.S.-Turkey citizen) and the injury of more activists and of IDF soldiers.

The incident is still controversial. Israeli sources argue that the Islamic İHH supports Hamas and has helped provide weapons and funds for "Islamic terrorist elements in the Middle East."[34] Flotilla activists accused Israeli commandos of immediately shooting; according to Israeli officials, the soldiers opened fire only after being attacked with clubs, knives, and a gun.[35] Several international investigations questioned the legality of Israel's blockade of Gaza and blamed Israel for the *Mavi Marmara* clash. However, a UN inquiry headed by Geoffrey Palmer published a report in September 2011 (delaying its findings reportedly to allow Israel and Turkey to continue reconciliation talks) that found the Israeli naval blockade of Gaza to be legal[36] and acknowledged that there were "serious questions about the conduct, true nature and objectives of the flotilla organizers, particularly IHH."[37]

Following several months of attempted reconciliation efforts, pushed vigorously by the U.S. government,[38] Turkey again downgraded its ties with Israel to the second secretary level, 30 years after the last downgrading (following the annexation of East Jerusalem).[39] Israel withdrew its ambassador to Turkey, and the two countries entered a six-year period of open and covert and track I and track II negotiations,[40] full of ups and downs and various crises and opportunities, until an agreement was reached in late June 2016.

---

[34] "Profile: Free Gaza Movement," *BBC News*, June 1, 2010.

[35] "Mavi Marmara: Why Did Israel Stop the Gaza Flotilla?" *BBC News*, June 27, 2016.

[36] R. Buchan, "II. The Palmer Report and the Legality of Israel's Naval Blockade Of Gaza," *International and Comparative Law Quarterly*, Vol. 61, No. 1, January 2012, pp. 264–273.

[37] Geoffrey Palmer, Alvaro Uribe, Joseph Ciechanover Itzhar, and Süleyman Özdem Sanberk, "Report of the Secretary-General's Panel of Inquiry on the 31 May 2010 Flotilla Incident," New York: United Nations, September 2, 2011.

[38] Dan Arbell, "The U.S.-Turkey-Israel Triangle," Washington, D.C., Brookings Institution, Analysis Paper Number 34, October 2014.

[39] A diplomatic rank at the officer level below the management level and several ranks below the ambassador.

[40] *Track I diplomacy* refers to official diplomatic contacts. Parties involved in *track II diplomacy*, also known as "backchannel diplomacy," are not official representatives of the conflicting sides but influential private citizens or groups of individuals.

CHAPTER THREE

Normalization Achieved After a Six-Year Process

The *Mavi Marmara* incident exacerbated an ongoing crisis in Israeli-Turkish relations that has damaged all levels of ties and influenced public opinion in both countries. Since the 2010 crisis, the United States attempted to broker a reconciliation of these two American allies; however, neither side was in a rush to make the first step. Turkey demanded three conditions for reconciliation—an Israeli apology, compensation for the *Mavi Marmara* victims, and the lifting of the blockade on Gaza. Of the three conditions, the apology did not come easy for Israel. An official with Israel's National Security Council (NSC) explained that

> The Obama Administration strongly pressured us to apologize and for three years we did not know what to say because we didn't want to apologize. It's not smart to apologize to someone like Erdoğan.[1]

Although Israel did not apologize, it embarked on several confidence-building measures in 2012–2013 that helped pave the way for later reconciliation. One such step was the sale of Israeli technology for upgrading the Turkish Air Force's early warning systems, a deal reportedly pushed by U.S. officials seeking to support reconciliation between the two countries.[2] In March 2013, then–President Barack Obama facilitated a telephone call between Netanyahu and Erdoğan and joined the call while visiting Israel; during the call, Netanyahu apologized and "agreed to complete the agreement for compensation," according to an official statement.[3] Turkey, for its part, agreed to cancel all the *Mavi Marmara*-related legal proceedings against IDF officers and soldiers. Further, the two leaders agreed to normalize relations and reinstate their

---

[1]   Discussion with Turkey expert at the Israeli National Security Council, Jerusalem, January 24, 2017.

[2]   Anshel Pfeffer, "Israel Supplies Turkey with Military Equipment for First Time Since Gaza Flotilla," *Haaretz*, February 18, 2013.

[3]   According to experts, substantial effort was involved in orchestrating the apology, including the telephone call itself and the exact wording used (email exchange with a Turkey scholar at an Israeli think tank, January 19, 2018).

respective ambassadors.[4] After the call, an official statement said that the United States "attache[s] great importance to the restoration of positive relations between them in order to advance regional peace and security."[5]

Negotiations continued, but while the two sides could narrow their differences,[6] the reconciliation process stagnated. Turkey insisted on lifting the Gaza blockade, and Israel demanded that Ankara shut down Hamas' offices in Turkey. Additional events prolonged the process. Protests in Turkey drew Erdoğan's attention to domestic affairs, and Israel was also worried about instability in Turkey, considering the instability in other countries in the region. Further, during July 2014's Operation Protective Edge in Gaza—the third war between Israel and Hamas since December 2008—dozens of Israelis and over 1,500 Palestinians were killed.[7] Israel's policies in Gaza once again caused the two sides to drift apart, with anti-Israel sentiment solidifying in Turkish public opinion.[8] In addition, Israel was put off by Erdoğan's continued inflammatory rhetoric that "[s]ounded as if came directly from Tehran."[9]

Several major shifts in the region since 2015 have helped facilitate the rapprochement between Israel and Turkey. The first are the countries' shared interests in stabilizing Syria, including mitigating adverse spillover effects and outcomes of the civil war. At the outset of the Syrian uprising, both governments advocated regime change, but they tempered this goal as it became clear that Assad was winning the civil war in Syria and that a complete collapse of the regime could cause wider instability.[10] Turkey and Israel have distinct long-term objectives in Syria. Turkey's highest priority is to prevent the Kurdish People's Protection Units (*Yekîneyên Parastina Gel*, or YPG), which it views as a terrorist group, from gaining control of a contiguous stretch of territory along its southern border as the YPG leads the efforts to defeat the Islamic State in

---

[4]   Herb Keinon, "Netanyahu Apologizes to Turkey over Gaza Flotilla," *Jerusalem Post*, March 22, 2013.

[5]   Joel Greenberg and Scott Wilson, "Obama Ends Israel Visit by Brokering End to Dispute with Turkey," *Washington Post*, March 22, 2013.

[6]   Nasi, 2017.

[7]   The UN estimated the number of Palestinian deaths at 2,133, of whom 1,489 were civilians. By contrast, Israeli estimates suggest that there were 1,598 Palestinian fatalities in Protective Edge, of whom 75 percent were combatants. See Raphael S. Cohen, David E. Johnson, David E. Thaler, Brenna Allen, Elizabeth M. Bartels, James Cahill, and Shira Efron, *Lessons from Israel's Wars in Gaza*, Santa Monica, Calif.: RAND Corporation, RR-1888-A, 2017.

[8]   While Turkish public opinion was already biased against Israel following previous rounds of violence in Gaza and the *Marmara* incident, anti-Israel rhetoric escalated severely in 2014; the Turkish Jewish community was targeted, and demonstrations near the Israeli embassy and consulates led the diplomatic delegations to reduce their staff to only several necessary members. See Gallia Lindenstrauss, "Operation Protective Edge: Deepening the Rift Between Israel and Turkey," in Anat Kurz and Shlomo Brom, eds., *The Lessons of Operation Protective Edge*, Tel Aviv: Institute for National Security Studies, 2014.

[9]   Discussion with a former Israeli diplomat who served in Turkey, Jerusalem, January 24, 2017.

[10]   Telephone discussion with an Israeli diplomat with Turkey expertise, March 1, 2017.

northern and eastern Syria. Turkey fears that a Kurdish autonomous region in Syria would provide another safe haven for terrorist operations into Turkey in the near term and a building block for an independent Kurdish state (encompassing parts of southeastern Turkey, Syria, Iraq, and Iran) over the long term. Israel wants to ensure that Iran and Hezbollah do not emerge with a stronghold along its northern border to sustain the "rejectionist front" against Israel.[11]

Second, Turkey and Israel have traditionally shared an anxiety over Iran. Several interlocutors indicated this feeling reached a new high in 2015, as Tehran could fulfill its regional aspirations in both Syria and Iraq. The nuclear agreement with Iran[12] and what had been perceived as a U.S. retreat from the region further exacerbated Israeli and Turkish, as well as Arab Sunni (Saudi, Emirati, Jordanian, and Egyptian) concerns. However, both of these interests that helped bring Israel and Turkey together in 2015–2016—a preferred outcome in Syria and a shared set of views on Iran—have changed as the Syrian war winds down.[13]

Non-security developments related to natural gas were the ultimate game changers leading to Israeli-Turkish reconciliation. From Turkey's perspective, the event that truly spurred its renewed ties with Israel was the downing of the Russian bomber that violated its airspace in November 2015. Russia provides Turkey approximately 60 percent of its gas and is also an important trade partner. The Turkish-Russian crisis reminded Turkey of the need to diversify its energy sources away from Russia and to seek other regional allies, opening the door back to Israel. Some Israeli officials agree that while shared regional interests with Turkey were important, the natural gas interest was the main catalyst for rapprochement.[14] They are convinced that the main advocate for renewal of ties was Energy Minister Yuval Steinitz.[15]

Steinitz's rationale was as follows. In December 2015, an international arbitration court ordered Cairo to pay a fine of almost $1.73 billion to Israel over gas that was supplied to Egypt through a Sinai pipeline. Following this decision, the Egyptian government ordered its oil and gas companies to freeze all business related to Israeli gas.[16] Worried about the loss of the Egyptian market for its newly discovered gas fields,

---

[11] Telephone discussion with an Israeli think tank analyst with Turkey expertise, January 25, 2017.

[12] An international agreement designed to set restrictions on Iran's nuclear program, signed in Vienna on July 14, 2015, between Iran, the five permanent members of the UN Security Council (China, France, Russia, United Kingdom, United States), Germany, and the European Union.

[13] Even though Israel and Turkey were united in their initial goals in Syria and suspicions toward Tehran, Ankara has been working with the Assad regime and its backers—Iran and Russia—on a quid pro quo in which Turkey would support a settlement on Damascus's terms as long as Kurdish autonomy is blunted.

[14] Discussion with official in the Israeli Ministry of Foreign Affairs, March 1, 2017.

[15] Discussion with official in the Israeli Ministry of Foreign Affairs, March 1, 2017; interview with an Israeli Turkey expert, Tel Aviv, January 25, 2017.

[16] See Tamim Elyan and Abdel Latif Wahba, "Egypt to Freeze Israeli Gas Import Talks After Court Ruling," *Bloomberg*, December 6, 2015.

Israel turned to the other potential large market in the region—Turkey. Less than ten days after the Egyptian announcement, Turkish and Israeli delegates signed a preliminary normalization deal, which included an agreement over a compensation fund of $20 million for the *Mavi Marmara* victims and the expulsion of a senior Turkey-based Hamas leader.[17]

In late June 2016, Turkey and Israel reconciled formally. The agreement stipulated that in addition to the *Mavi Marmara* compensation, Israel would enable Turkey to set up infrastructure projects in Gaza (e.g., a hospital, a power station, a desalination facility). All the materials for these projects would be transported via Israel's Ashdod Port. According to an Israeli scholar of Turkey, Ankara presented this as an achievement, although it could have always supported Gaza as long as it shipped goods through Ashdod and met Israel's security requirements.[18]

Israel's immediate gain from the agreement, in addition to rapprochement with a longtime ally, was that Turkey lifted the veto it put during the crisis years on any North Atlantic Treaty Organization (NATO)–Israel collaboration, and just before the signing of the agreement Israel opened a representative office in NATO.[19] In addition, Turkey committed to passing a law that would bar and prevent claims against IDF personnel, vowed that Hamas would not carry out any terrorist or military activity against Israel from Turkish territory, and promised to seek the return of two Israeli citizens and the remains of two soldiers held in Gaza.

Turkey waived its requirement that Israel remove the blockade of Gaza, and Israel came to terms with continued Hamas presence in Turkey. Pragmatism and shared interests made both parties set aside some of their demands—the exact demands that had forestalled the reconciliation for six years.[20]

---

[17] Nasi, 2017.

[18] Email exchange with an Israel journalist and scholar of Turkey, March 1, 2017.

[19] Herb Keinon, "Israel to Open Permanent Office at NATO HQ Five Years After Turkey Blocked Move," *Jerusalem Post*, May 4, 2016.

[20] "All You Need to Know About the Israel-Turkey Reconciliation," *Haaretz*, June 27, 2016.

CHAPTER FOUR

Post-Rapprochement Economic Relations

Israel and Turkey have, for the most part, been able to separate economic from strategic-security relations. Still, the normalization of ties in 2016 represented an important milestone, moving toward enabling expansion of potential economic cooperation, especially in tourism, trade, and energy. However, despite mutual interests, greater economic cooperation between Israel and Turkey could be hindered for two key reasons. First, some of the key incentives, including economic incentives, that brought the two countries together in 2016 have dissipated. Further, despite potential mutual benefits, political obstacles (discussed in Chapter Five) generate additional risks that could disincentivize further cooperation. In May 2018, commentators in Israel warned that the diplomatic feud with Turkey could also harm economic ties between the two countries.[1]

Israeli-Turkish Trade Has Been Growing Despite Political Divides

Despite the diplomatic freeze between Israel and Turkey between 2010 and 2016, bilateral trade increased during those years.[2] However, according to 2016 data, there has been a decrease in the number of Israeli companies operating in Turkey, and 33 percent of the Israeli companies that operated in Turkey before the flotilla have stopped working there.[3] That could be explained by tensions affecting both sides—Israeli investors viewed Turkey as risky, fearing instability and an anti-Israel climate. Turkish businesspeople have told Israeli counterparts that during the crisis years, they were waiting for a "green light" from the government to do business in Israel. As one official noted,

---

[1]   Sami Peretz, "An Angry Erdogan Stands to Harm Israel-Turkey Economic Ties, *Haaretz*, May 17, 2018.

[2]   "Turkish-Israeli Economic, Trade Ties Expected to Soar After Deal," *Hurriyet Daily News*, June 27, 2016.

[3]   Yuval Azulay, "Machon Ha'Yetzu: Ha'Piyus Im Turkkya Yiten 'Boost' Nosaf Le'Kishrey Ha'Sachar," *Globes*, June 27, 2016.

"While it was not formally forbidden, Turks did not feel comfortable working with Israelis while their leader is saying that Israelis are murderers and child killers."[4]

Following the normalization of ties, trade has been on the rise. In 2017, Israel was one of the ten most important export markets for Turkey. Turkish exports to Israel reached $4.3 billion in 2016, and the first 11 months of 2017 saw a further substantial increase.[5] Turkey is interested in continued expansion of trade, as the AKP has a strong economic agenda and Erdoğan pursues the advancement of Turkish business interests as a high priority. Thus, the Israeli market matters.[6] From Israel's perspective, Turkey is a large and important market with 75 million potential consumers. It is Israel's fifth largest trading partner after the United States, the United Kingdom, China, and the Netherlands.[7] Israeli economists estimate the potential bilateral trade at $8 billion per year,[8] approximately twice the 2016 amount.

One Israeli economic interest is completing an aviation agreement that would open the Turkish aviation market to Israeli airlines. There are nine to 11 flights per day from Tel Aviv to Turkey, none of which is by an Israeli carrier. While Israel's national airline, El Al, flew to Turkey until 2007, no Israeli carriers have flown there since—leaving them without access to Istanbul, an important global aviation hub. Meanwhile, Turkish Airlines is the second largest airline (after El Al) in Israel's national Ben Gurion Airport in terms of number of flights. An initial agreement, which was drafted on this matter in 2009, was tabled after the *Mavi Marmara* crisis and then revisited. Despite reaching understandings, Israeli carriers remain locked out of the Turkish market, mostly over security issues; in 2007, Turkey stopped ceding to Israeli security demands and does not want armed Israeli personnel conducting security checks in its airport.[9] Resuming flights to Turkey by Israeli carriers would provide substantial economic benefits for Israel.[10]

Turkey also has an interest in establishing Qualifying Industrial Zones (QIZs) with Israel, like the QIZs that exist in Egypt and Jordan. (QIZs are industrial parks that house manufacturing operations and were established to take advantage of the free trade agreements between the United States and Israel.) One Israeli MFA official opposes the establishment of an Israeli-Turkish QIZ at this stage, however, seeing it as a benefit only to be conveyed in exchange for progress with Turkey on the aviation

---

[4] Telephone discussion with an Israeli MFA official, March 1, 2017.

[5] "Turkish Businesspeople Seek Trade Boost with Israel," *Anadolu Agency*, November 27, 2017; "Turkey and Israel: Animosity Ends When It Comes to Money," *Deutsche Welle*, December 12, 2017.

[6] Sharon Udasin, "Turkish Industrial Leaders Call for Trade Increase with Israel," *Jerusalem Post*, May 16, 2017.

[7] Ramzi Gabai, "Lenatzel et Hamomentum Hachiyuvi," *Marker Magazine*, March 1, 2017 [translated from Hebrew].

[8] Telephone discussion with an Israeli MFA official, March 1, 2017.

[9] Raphael Ahren, "In Battle for the Skies, Turkey Beats Israel 112:0," *Times of Israel*, October 31, 2013.

[10] Telephone discussion with an Israeli MFA official, March 1, 2017.

agreement or restraint in its Palestinian engagement. While the Turkish government has not sought to reinitiate discussions over QIZs since 2016, the Israelis anticipate that Turkey will seek Israeli help in convincing a reluctant U.S. Congress to approve pro-Turkish steps, such as the QIZ concept.[11] This prospect, however, had diminished by late 2017, due to strains in U.S.-Turkish relations.

Normalization Has Helped Boost Israeli Tourism to Turkey

One area of improvement in Israeli-Turkish relations post-rapprochement is tourism. Israeli tourism to Turkey did not stop entirely during the crisis years, but per Turkish statistics, it did plunge to 80,000 visitors per year in the worst times (after the *Mavi Marmara* incident; by 2013, the number had increased to 164,917). In 2016, prior to that year's reconciliation, 200,000 Israelis visited Turkey; the number jumped to 293,988 by the end of that year.[12] While Israeli tourism to Turkey is relatively small compared with tourism from countries like Germany and Russia (in better times, 560,000 Israelis visited Turkey annually, compared with millions of visitors from Germany and Russia), it is important for certain resort areas that have traditionally drawn most Israeli visitors. In May 2017, almost a year after the reconciliation, an official delegation headed by Antalya's governor visited Israel with the aim of reviving Israeli tourism to that province, which was Israel's most popular vacation destination in the previous decade. While 170,000 Israelis visited Antalya in 2016, this figure is still half of the 330,000 visitors in 2008, prior to the crisis.[13]

The reason for the slow growth of tourism to Turkey may be related less to the state of bilateral relations and more to security concerns after a series of attacks hit Turkey in 2015–2016.[14] A March 2016 attack targeting Israelis on a culinary tour caused three Israeli fatalities. Another Israeli citizen, an Arab Israeli teenager, was killed in the terrorist attack in an Istanbul nightclub on December 31, 2016.[15] Consequently, Israel's Counter-Terrorism Bureau issued a severe formal travel warning to Turkey cautioning against possible terror attacks and kidnap attempts and urging Israelis in Turkey to leave the country.[16] In response, Turkish ambassador to Israel Kemal Ökem said that

---

[11] Telephone discussion with an Israeli MFA official, March 1, 2017.

[12] Daniel K. Eisenbud, "Turkey Remains Popular Tourist Destination for Israeli Arabs," *Jerusalem Post*, January 1, 2017; "Israeli Tourists Flock to Turkey As Relations Normalize, Number of Tourists Rise 80 Percent," *Daily Sabah* and *Anadolu Agency*, February 5, 2017.

[13] Amir Alon, "Turkish Ambassador to Israel Trying to Coax Israelis Back to Antalya," *Ynet News*, May 25, 2017.

[14] Alon, 2017.

[15] Erin Cunningham and Kareem Fahim, "Slain Partiers Came to Istanbul from Near and Far to Celebrate the New Year," *The Washington Post*, January 1, 2017.

[16] Itamar Eichner, "Israel Issues Travel Warning for Turkey, Jordan and Egypt," *Ynet News*, March 27, 2017.

Turkey guarantees the security of all visiting Israelis and that Turkey is just as safe as any other place in Europe.[17]

Tourism data for 2017 were not available at time of writing (December 2017); however, news reports indicate that Israeli tourism to Turkey is growing, although at a slower rate than anticipated and not among all sectors of Israeli society. While Turkey was historically the most popular vacation destination among Israelis, it now faces a competition from other affordable nearby markets, such as Greece and Cyprus, which have become more popular among Israel's Jewish majority.[18] As of late 2017, most Israeli tourists to Turkey are Arab Israelis (21 percent of the Israeli population, or 1.8 million people).[19]

Turkey, for its part, wants Israel to make it easier for Turkish citizens to travel to Israel. However, Israel is not likely to do so, as security risk assessments concerning Turkish citizens visiting Israel have not changed dramatically after the normalization agreement.[20] From the Israeli perspective, there is a concrete concern that some Turks would cause provocations on the Temple Mount. Indeed, as discussed in more detail in Chapter Five, Israel is worried about Turkish religious activism in Jerusalem and has even barred the entrance of Turkish worshippers, wearing shirts with the Turkish flags, to the Temple Mount.[21]

While Turks do not visit Israel in large numbers, as a result of the civil war in Syria, the Haifa port turned into a key transit point for Turkish exports to Jordan, which could no longer be shipped by truck through Syria. Some 30–40 trucks and their drivers arrive in freighters to the port every week, and from there they drive through Israel to Jordan.[22]

Strong, Albeit Waning, Bilateral Interest in Energy Trade

As noted earlier, potential energy collaboration was a strong incentive for the rapprochement between Israel and Turkey. Israel has historically relied on imports to satisfy its energy needs, but in 2009, the discovery of the first natural gas field, Tamar, in its coastal waters changed the picture. Tamar supplies more than half of Israel Electrical Corporation's needs, providing power to Israel and the PA. In 2010, the discovery of the Leviathan field, which is estimated to hold 470 to 620 billion cubic meters

---

[17]   Alon, 2017.

[18]   Michal Raz-Chaimovich, "Israeli Vacationers Desert Eilat for Cyprus," *Globes*, August 21, 2017.

[19]   Eisenbud, 2017.

[20]   Telephone discussion with an Israeli think tank analyst with Turkey expertise, January 25, 2017.

[21]   Nadav Shargai, "Ha'Pe Shel Erdoğan, Ha'Milim Shel Hamas," *Israel Hayom*, December 28, 2017.

[22]   Peretz, 2018.

(BCM), was considered a game changer, transforming Israel to a potential energy-exporting country.[23] Utilizing the potential of Leviathan depends on developing the field, which could cost some $4 billion.[24] This large investment in turn hinges on identifying a substantial export market in the region—a prospect constrained by Israel's geopolitical situation.[25]

One agreement was developed to sell Jordan 45 BCM over ten years, but the Jordanian market is very limited.[26] On February 19, 2018, the gas partnerships in Israel announced a $15 billion contract to export 64 BCM of natural gas to Egypt over ten years. The multinationals in Egypt seek to buy Israeli gas, liquefy it in Egyptian facilities, and then export it to Europe.[27] Doubts surfaced immediately regarding implementation of this deal, as Egyptian officials indicated that they are not interested in further energy deals with Israel after a ruling by an international court on debt payment.[28] In addition, in 2015, the massive gas field Zohr, containing 900 BCM, was discovered in Egypt's territorial waters, making it hard for Israel to compete in Egypt's domestic market.[29] As mentioned earlier, some analysts have proposed that Israel build an undersea pipeline to connect to Europe via Cyprus and Greece, but this option might be commercially unrealistic.[30]

A Feasible Deal or a Pipe Dream?

In 2015–2016, in contrast to other potential markets in the region, Turkey seemed like an ideal candidate, both technically and financially. Turkey imports almost all of its natural gas, almost 60 percent from Russia and 20 percent from Iran, and wanted to diversify away from these two sources, especially after the crisis in Turkish-Russian relations in 2015. A prominent Turkish energy expert was quoted in the press explaining that Israeli gas can help Turkey meet its energy demands and help it diversify away from Russian sources, creating "a win-win situation for the two countries."[31]

---

[23]   University of Haifa and the Hudson Institute, *Report of the Commission on the Eastern Mediterranean*, September 2016.

[24]   Interview with prominent Israeli energy expert, Herzliya, January 22, 2017.

[25]   Gabriel Mitchell, "The Risks and Rewards of Israeli-Turkish Energy Cooperation," Israel Turkey Policy Dialogue Publication Series, Global Political Trends Center, Istanbul Kultur University, and Mitvim, January 2017.

[26]   "Israel Consortium Signs 'Historic' 15-Year, $10b Gas Deal with Jordan," *Times of Israel*, September 26, 2016.

[27]   Oded Eran, Elai Rettig, and Ofir Winter, "The Gas Deal with Egypt: Israel Deepens Its Anchor in the Eastern Mediterranean," *INSS Insight*, No. 1033, March 12, 2018.

[28]   David Rosenberg, "Why Isn't Egypt Joining Israel's Natural Gas Deal Party?" *Haaretz*, February 20, 2018.

[29]   Hedy Cohen, "Egypt's Zohr Gas Reservoir Estimate Keeps Growing," *Globes*, July 25, 2016.

[30]   Elias Hazou, "'Tripartite' Gas Would Be Double the Price, Experts Say," *Cyprus Mail Online*, February 7, 2016.

[31]   Hedy Cohen, "Eni's Egypt Gas Find Limits Israel's Gas Export Options," *Globes*, September 1, 2015.

In addition to benefits for Turkey, proponents of such a deal argue that the value for the Israeli economy could be substantial. Furthermore, Israeli advocates see the deal as a feasible means to enable the development of the Leviathan field—which they consider a national security strategic interest. Per a prominent energy expert, Israel's dependence on the Tamar gasfield, which supplies 60 percent of its needs, is an enormous strategic risk, as "any technical failure somewhere along the chain could shut down the power."[32] During Operation Protective Edge in Gaza in 2014, Hamas fired rockets at the Tamar field platforms.[33] Although Israel has recently deployed the sea-based version of the Iron Dome system,[34] the dependence on Tamar and its associated installations creates a dangerous Israeli vulnerability. Back-up gas sources, such as Leviathan, are needed, but given the small size of the Israeli market, their development is linked to the Turkish route.[35]

Skeptics cast doubts on the viability of exporting Israeli gas to Turkey for a variety of reasons. First, it is not clear that Turkey's interest in diversifying from Russian gas remains as strong. Since the 2015 rift, Moscow and Ankara reconciled, and experts believe that the reconciliation was prompted in part by Putin's interest in keeping Turkey overdependent on Russian gas. In fact, Turkish-Russian ties have improved substantially since late 2017, as both countries have been collaborating in shaping the aftermath of the Syrian war.[36] Improved diplomatic ties have implications also for the energy dimension, as the two countries are seeking broader energy collaboration, specifically on the TurkStream gas pipeline from Russia to Turkey and the Akkuyu nuclear power plant, being built in Turkey in collaboration with Russia.[37] Moreover, it is not clear that gas exported from Israel would be able to compete with Russian gas. In an effort to preserve its Turkish market share, it is projected that Gazprom will further reduce the price to a rate that Israel would not be able to match.[38]

There are also cost and technical difficulties. Constructing an undersea pipeline from Israel to Turkey is a complicated endeavor that would take several years and cost an estimated $2 billion to $4 billion.[39] Securing and protecting such a pipeline is also

---

[32]   Conversation with prominent Israeli energy expert, Herzliya, January 22, 2017.

[33]   Simon Henderson, "A Hamas Rocket Hitting Israeli Gas Platforms Could Re-Escalate the Gaza War," *Business Insider*, August 21, 2014.

[34]   "Israel has Deployed Its Iron Dome Missile-Defense System on Ships for First Time," Associated Press, November 28, 2017.

[35]   Interview with prominent Israeli energy expert, Herzliya, January 22, 2017.

[36]   Dorian Jones, "Turkey Hosts Iranian, Russian FMs as Ankara-NATO Dispute Festers," *Voice of America*, November 19, 2017.

[37]   Radio Free Europe, December 2017.

[38]   The Israeli governmental gas development plan guaranteed that Israel would not export gas at a lower price than is charged domestically.

[39]   Mitchell, 2017.

a major challenge. Moreover, pipeline infrastructure for transporting gas inside Turkey would require an additional \$2 billion to \$3 billion, an unlikely investment without long-term contracts and guarantees.[40] Considering the decrease in energy rates over the past few years, these costs might deter investments in exorbitant gas projects, especially considering the political risks borne out of the tense political relations between Israel and Turkey and the latter's overall declining position in the U.S.-NATO spheres. As the diplomatic rift over the Palestinian casualties in Gaza and the opening of the U.S. embassy in Jerusalem demonstrated, Israeli-Turkish ties will continue to face crises, most likely over the Palestinian issue.[41] In that event, what would happen if Turkey decides to cancel all agreements with Israel? There are mechanisms to hedge against such risks (including political risk insurance), but according to officials, investors and banks are hesitant about investing in and lending to initiatives that may depend eventually on Erdoğan's good will.[42]

Finally, a major obstacle to the construction of an Israeli-Turkish pipeline is Cyprus. Cypriot officials have repeatedly argued that they would not allow a pipeline to go through their economic waters unless the conflict with Turkey is resolved,[43] a prospect that is not promising in the short term. While it is not clear whether Cyprus can block the deal and the construction of the pipeline—Turkey says it cannot, but Cyprus disagrees[44]—all agree that it can delay it, and a delay in this case could have serious implications. Turkey has asked Israel to influence Cyprus in favor of the deal.[45] On the opposing side, Russia has substantial influence in Cyprus and may use it to pressure the Cypriot government to slow the approval process on the pipeline to benefit Moscow.[46] Up until late 2017, Israel and Turkey said that they were planning to build the pipeline by the end of 2019, expecting it to carry gas in 2021, which is when Turkey's existing gas contract with Russia expires. If Cyprus holds back the deal using

---

[40]   Interview with prominent Israeli energy expert, Herzliya, January 22, 2017.

[41]   Benjamin Harvey, "Erdogan Says He'd Cut Israel Ties If Trump Acts on Jerusalem," *Bloomberg*, December 5, 2017.

[42]   An Israeli diplomat explained that "the actual agreement will be within the private sector, and that will be much harder to cancel. If one government wants to cancel, it'll have to compensate the companies involved. However, if it ends up being the national Turkish gas company, then Ankara can tell them that they would compensate them in the future and immediately terminate the deal. If that is where things are heading, it should serve as a strong warning sign." Telephone interview with an Israeli MFA official, March 1, 2017.

[43]   Michele Kambas, "Cyprus Blocks Israel-Turkey Gas Pipeline Until Ankara Mends Ties," *Haaretz*, July 6, 2016.

[44]   Selcan Hacaoglu, "Turkey Lobbying Israel to Push Cyprus on Approving Gas Pipeline," *Bloomberg*, July 20, 2017.

[45]   Telephone interview with an Israeli MFA official, March 1, 2017.

[46]   Sara Stefanini, "Cyprus Fears Russia Could Wreck Reunification," *Politico*, January 12, 2017.

legal proceedings, the critical 2021 deadline could be missed.[47] Other analysts, however, explain that Cyprus may not pose such an obstacle to the deal but would just seek to ensure that its own newly discovered gas field gets connected to the Israel-Turkey pipeline.[48]

In any event, a possible Israel-Turkey gas deal has serious implications for Israel's ties with Cyprus, which Israel views as extremely important. As described in more detail in Chapter Five, ties with both Cyprus and Greece were transformed after Israeli-Turkish relations soured following the *Mavi Marmara* incident, filling a gap in Israel's regional strategy.[49] Even as it mends fences with Turkey, Israel has been working to maintain strong relations with both Greece and Cyprus and is paying special attention to the possible ramifications of a potential gas deal.

Turkey and Israel are at least formally still exploring a joint gas deal. In February 2017, developers of Leviathan approved a $3.75 billion investment.[50] According to the developers, a new 300-mile pipeline could be conveying Israeli gas to Turkey by the end of 2020.[51] Further, on July 12, 2017, the Deputy Consul General of Israel in Istanbul tweeted that Steinitz said that he and his Turkish counterpart, Minister of Energy and Natural Resources Berat Albayrak, planned to "accelerate the talks and sign an agreement by the end of the year."[52]

However, as of January 2018, a deal had not been signed.[53] In addition, Israel is still examining the feasibility of alternative agreements that would not involve Turkey.[54] In early December 2017, Israel signed an agreement with Cyprus, Greece, and Italy on the EastMed Pipeline Project, a potential undersea pipeline carrying natural gas from deposits in the eastern Mediterranean, including Leviathan, to Europe.[55] The feasibility of this alternative project, however, as mentioned earlier, remains questionable.[56]

---

[47] Telephone discussion with an Israeli diplomat, March 1, 2017.

[48] "Turkey Sees No Need for Cyprus to Approve Israel Gas Pipeline," *Bloomberg*, April 13, 2017.

[49] Discussion with Turkey expert at the Israeli National Security Council, Jerusalem, January 24, 2017.

[50] Tova Cohen and Ari Rabinovitch, "Leviathan Gas Field Developers Approve $3.75 Billion Investment," *Reuters*, February 23, 2017.

[51] "Israel-Turkey Gas Pipeline Could Be Ready in Four Years—Company," *Reuters*, March 2, 2017.

[52] Shira Ben Tzion, Twitter post, 1:24 AM, July 12, 2017.

[53] "Israel Expects Gas to Flow from East Mediterranean to Europe," 2017.

[54] Discussion with Israeli MFA officials, Jerusalem, December 13, 2017.

[55] "Israel Expects Gas to Flow from East Mediterranean to Europe," 2017.

[56] Simone Tagliapietra, "Is the Eastmed Gas Pipeline Just Another EU Pipe Dream?" *Bruegel*, May 10, 2017.

Conclusion

Israel and Turkey have mutual economic interests, including trade, tourism, and energy. Historically, Israel and Turkey have been able to separate their economic interests from their political and diplomatic differences, as evidenced in the continuation and expansion of bilateral trade even during the crisis years of 2010 to 2016. At the same time, from Israel's perspective, developments during these years have led to the emergence of several alternatives to Turkey—in tourism, trade, and possibly even in energy cooperation. In addition, the formal Israeli-Turkish rapprochement has not brought the two countries much closer, and political risks remain to both sides given the threat that relations could sour further—a risk that is explored in detail in subsequent chapters. This political risk, combined with the existence of alternatives such as Cyprus and Greece, means that the strong economic potential of ties between Israel and Turkey may not easily be fulfilled. Considering the political atmosphere between Turkey and Israel, it would only be feasible to separate business from politics and continue strengthening economic cooperation if the war of words were to abate, which is likely unrealistic in the current climate.

CHAPTER FIVE

Diplomatic and Security Relations After Normalization

In contrast to the economic sphere, where Israel and Turkey have strong, albeit still unfulfilled, potential, Israel and Turkey are clearly divided on political and diplomatic issues. Indeed, their ties have always been affected by ups and downs in the Israeli-Arab peace process, and that remains the case today. However, the two former allies no longer necessarily see eye-to-eye on issues that previously were of common interest. This chapter discusses the main points of contention between Israel and Turkey on the diplomatic front, starting with the Palestinian issue, in which tensions are centered on Gaza, Jerusalem, and the AKP's support for Hamas. In addition, the chapter analyzes divergent objectives in Syria, differences on the question of Kurdish independence, and Israel's new ties with Greece and Cyprus. I also discuss the prospects for renewed defense ties. Politically and security-wise, Israel and Turkey have drifted apart substantially since the late 2000s and throughout the crisis years. Their differences concerning the Palestinians are as deep as ever, fueling tensions that culminated in May 2018 in the two countries expelling each other's envoys. Although regional developments helped bring Turkey and Israel together again in 2016, events in Syria since then have pushed their objectives in different directions. Due to these divisions and a general Israeli mistrust of Erdoğan's Turkey, resumption of security cooperation, once the bedrock of ties, is unlikely.

Divisions on the Palestinian Issue Make Political Ties Most Precarious

Turkish-Palestinian relations are longstanding and complex, partly as a result of the 400-year Ottoman rule in Palestine preceding the British Mandate. While Turkey has remained a champion of the Palestinian cause over the years, it has often had to balance its positions carefully, given its close ties with Israel. Ups and downs in Israeli-Turkish relations have always been linked to developments on the Israeli-Palestinian front. This was true before the AKP came to power, but escalation has become quicker and more intense under the AKP rule.[1] Intra-Palestinian factional rivalry between the

---

[1]   Interview with an Israeli Turkey expert, Tel Aviv, January 25, 2017.

Fatah-led PA and Hamas has further complicated Turkish-Palestinian relations and added another layer of complexity to the Turkey-Israel-Palestinian triangle. Turkish-Israeli disagreements on the Palestinian issue concern two main arenas—Gaza and East Jerusalem. The IDF killing dozens of Palestinians in violent protests in Gaza—which was linked with the opening of the U.S. embassy in Jerusalem in May 2018—hit those two exposed nerves.

Divisions Alongside Shared Objectives in Gaza

During the 2011–2016 diplomatic rift, one of the key Turkish demands was to lift the Gaza blockade.[2] Israel, from its perspective, demanded that Turkey stop sheltering leaders of Hamas's military wing in its territory. Even though Turkey expelled some Hamas military leaders, Israel is worried that this demand has not entirely been met. The AKP ties with Hamas, and its affiliated movement, the Muslim Brotherhood, are strong, longstanding, and multifaceted. These ties are worrisome to Israel and other countries in the region, especially Egypt and Jordan, because they reflect shared ideology and desire to assert a Turkish dominance in the region.[3] In addition to ideological common ground, Israeli press reports that members of Hamas's military wing continue to operate in Turkey and that despite its commitment as part of the 2016 agreement, "Turkey is unsuccessful, or not trying hard enough, or perhaps even choosing to ignore Hamas activity in its territory."[4] According to officials in the Israeli NSC, Hamas receives financial support from organizations affiliated with the AKP.[5] Turkey has at times been able to separate its ideological ties with Hamas from its interests in ties with Israel but has linked the issues at other times. Considering that fighting between Israel and Hamas is considered just a matter of time,[6] growing tensions between Israel and Turkey over this issue are likely.

Interestingly, despite the ideological divides, Israel and Turkey share some objectives on Gaza. Both countries want to prevent a humanitarian disaster there, and Israel welcomes Turkey's reconstruction efforts. Turkey's support includes building a new hospital, cleaning water wells, constructing housing units, and shipping humanitar-

---

[2] It is worth noting that Turkey was somewhat vague in this demand, and experts were unsure whether it required the lifting of the naval blockade (which Israel adamantly refused) or easing access and movement through the land crossings (the main access points to Gaza already and an area where Israel was willing to show much more flexibility); based on an email exchange with a Turkey expert at an Israeli think tank, January 19, 2018.

[3] Mohammad Abdel Kader, "Turkey's Relationship with the Muslim Brotherhood," *Al Arabiya Institute for Studies*, October 14, 2013.

[4] Shargai, 2017.

[5] Shargai, 2017.

[6] Amos Harel, "No One Wants a War in Gaza, but the First Israeli Casualty Could Change Everything," *Haaretz*, January 5, 2018.

ian aid (including fuel)[7] through Israel's port of Ashdod. The Turkish Directorate of Religious Affairs (*Diyanet*) renovates mosques in Gaza,[8] and Turkey had planned to collaborate with Germany to build a power plant in Gaza.[9] Despite these efforts, some Israeli experts think that Turkey's assistance to Gaza is less ambitious than its pre-reconciliation promises.[10] Even if more limited than envisaged, presumably because it has been stretched thin on the Syrian front, Turkey's aid to Gaza has been substantial. Israel seeks to prevent further deterioration of living conditions in Gaza and welcomes Turkey's assistance. At the same time, however, Israel is worried that too much support would strengthen Hamas's position in the Palestinian arena and undermine the PA, which has been Israel's negotiation and security partner.

Israel is not the only country concerned over Turkish involvement in Gaza. Egypt—which in 2016 sought clarifications on the reconciliation talks with Turkey—has its own redlines.[11] Egypt vetoed Turkish construction of a Gaza port because it would be considered an ultimate prize for Hamas, granting the organization a symbol of sovereignty over Gaza. In addition, Egypt opposes any other Turkish political involvement in the Palestinian sphere, including Gaza. From Cairo's perspective, Erdoğan's and the AKP's deep ties with the Muslim Brotherhood disqualify them from any political role in the region, including in Gaza.[12] Given the central role Cairo assumed in fall 2017 attempting to mediate between the PA and Hamas, and the possible opening of Egypt's border crossing with Gaza,[13] Turkey's involvement in assisting Gaza could also depend on its relationship with Cairo, which was described by a former senior Palestinian official as "bad as can be. Erdoğan behaves as if Morsi is still the president, and Cairo wants an apology from Turkey."[14]

The Turkish response to the May 2018 clashes in Gaza, in which the IDF killed dozens of Palestinians and injured over 2,000, demonstrates that Gaza remains a point

---

[7]   Avi Issacharoff, "Hamas Says Turkey to Send Fuel to End Gaza Electricity Crisis," *Times of Israel*, January 14, 2017.

[8]   "Turkey Rebuilds 9 Mosques in Gaza," *Anadolu Agency*, November 15, 2016.

[9]   Although it is not clear yet whether this plan is being implemented. See "Israel and Turkey Normalization Deal Signed," *Globes*, June 28, 2016.

[10]   An Israeli journalist and scholar of Turkey explained that "It is true, though, that under the new framework Turkey can do much more for the Gazans in terms of infrastructure, water, and humanitarian supply than it did until now. Since the agreement, however, it seems that Ankara has lost its appetite to help" (email exchange, March 1, 2017).

[11]   Barak Ravid, "Egypt Asks Israel to Keep Turkey away from Gaza," *Haaretz*, January 7, 2016.

[12]   Interview with an Israeli Turkey expert, Tel Aviv, January 25, 2017.

[13]   During the time of writing, the Fatah-dominated PA and Hamas have been working to implement a reconciliation agreement that they signed in early October 2017, owing to Egyptian mediation. Reconciliation in the long term is expected to be challenging, however, as the fundamental differences between the Palestinian factions remain.

[14]   Telephone interview with a former senior Palestinian official, April 28, 2017.

of contention. Erdoğan said that "Netanyahu is the PM of an apartheid state . . . . He has the blood of Palestinians on his hands and can't cover up crimes by attacking Turkey." Netanyahu replied:

> A man who sends thousands of Turkish soldiers to hold the occupation of Northern Cyprus and invades Syria will not preach to us when we defend ourselves from an attempt by Hamas. A man whose hands are stained with the blood of countless Kurdish citizens in Turkey and Syria is the last person to preach to us about combat ethics.[15]

While other countries (e.g., Ireland, South Africa, Belgium) summoned the Israeli ambassadors for clarification on the death toll in Gaza, and several others condemned the violence and asked Israel to "exercise restraint,"[16] the diplomatic retaliation and the vehement rhetoric between the two countries suggest that this issue could lead to another serious diplomatic crisis.

Focus of Turkish Activity on Palestinian Front Has Shifted to Jerusalem

While Gaza was Turkey's explicit reason for downgrading ties with Israel and not reconciling earlier, analysts say Turkey is more focused on the question of East Jerusalem. The Turkish media constantly discusses Jerusalem, spreading a narrative that Israel seeks to change the status quo in Jerusalem and in the *Haram al-Sharif* (the area around Temple Mount, which is a holy site to Muslims). Erdoğan, perhaps more than any other Muslim leader, was vocal in his opposition to the U.S. recognition of Jerusalem as Israel's capital. He called for the emergency meeting of the Organization of the Islamic Conference in Istanbul following the announcement and said that he intends to open a Turkish embassy in East Jerusalem soon.[17] Turkey recalled its ambassadors to the United States and Israel after the May 2018 opening of the embassy and the deadly protests in Gaza. It is worth noting that Turkey already has a consulate in East Jerusalem predating the founding of the state of Israel, with a head of mission at the ambassador level; the Israelis expelled the consul there in retaliation for the expulsion of the Israeli ambassador to Turkey.[18]

In addition to its rhetoric, Turkey is also politically active in supporting Islamic groups in East Jerusalem.[19] During Erdoğan's tenure, he has increased Turkey's involve-

---

[15] Noa Landau and Jonathan Lis, "Turkey and Israel Expel Envoys over Gaza Deaths," *Haaretz*, May 16, 2018.

[16] Landau and Lis, 2018.

[17] Dorian Jones, "Turkey Summit Blasts Trump Decision on Jerusalem," *Voice of America*, December 13, 2017; "Erdogan Says Turkey Aims to Open Embassy in East Jerusalem," Reuters, December 17, 2017.

[18] Raphael Ahren, "Israel Expels Turkish Consul in Jerusalem After Ankara Boots Israel's Ambassador," *Times of Israel*, May 15, 2018.

[19] Telephone discussion with a Turkey expert at an Israeli think tank, January 25, 2017.

ment in East Jerusalem and the Muslim holy sites, primarily the Al-Aqsa Mosque. He also has strengthened ties with Palestinians citizens and residents of the state of Israel, including with the Northern Branch of the Islamic Movement, an affiliate of the Muslim Brotherhood that is outlawed in Israel.[20] In May 2017, less than a year after the reconciliation, Erdoğan lashed out at Israel after the Israeli parliament's preliminary approval of a bill restricting early morning Muslim calls to prayer, saying:

> Turkey attaches great importance to the justified resistance of the Palestinians and will not yield to Israeli attempts to change the status quo in the Al-Aqsa Mosque. We as Muslims should visit the Al-Aqsa Mosque more often, every day that Jerusalem is under occupation is an insult to us.[21]

To Israeli ears, these statements sounded like pre-rapprochement rhetoric. While historically Israel has refrained from responding to Turkish insults to avoid further escalation, the post-normalization policy is to answer with spite. According to Israeli experts, since the restraint policy has not been effective, rhetorical rebuffs are now seen as a possible means to stop Turkish verbal attacks. This strategy involves pungent attacks against Erdoğan personally.[22] Whether this new policy is successful is not yet clear.[23]

A terrorist attack on the Temple Mount on July 14, 2017, and Israel's response—closing the site for worshipers and installing metal detectors at several entrances (which were removed later due to international pressure)—led to further escalation in Israeli-Turkish tensions over Jerusalem.[24] Turkish Deputy Prime Minister Numan Kurtulmuş called Israel's temporary closure of the Temple Mount "a crime against humanity." Speaking at an AKP party meeting in parliament, Erdoğan called on Muslims to defend Al-Aqsa Mosque and said, "When Israeli soldiers carelessly pollute the grounds of Al-Aqsa with their combat boots by using simple issues as a pretext and then easily spill blood there, the reason is we [Muslims] have not done enough to stake our claim over Jerusalem."[25] The Israeli MFA responded again, attacking Erdoğan personally:

---

[20] David Koren and Ben Avrahami, "The Residents of Eastern Jerusalem at a Historic Crossroads," *Ha'Shiloach*, July 30, 2017.

[21] Eyal Lehman and Roi Kais, "Erdoğan Rebukes Israel over Muezzin Bill and Calls on Muslims to Go En Masse to Al-Aqsa," *Ynet*, May 8, 2017.

[22] Perhaps the first implementation of this new policy came in response to Erdoğan's May 2017 rebukes, only 11 months after the reconciliation, when the Israeli MFA issued a statement, saying that "[h]e who systematically violates human rights in his country will not preach morality to the only true democracy in the region" (Lehman and Kais, 2017).

[23] Email exchange with an Israeli think tank expert on Turkey, January 19, 2018.

[24] Isabel Kershner, "Israel Agrees to Remove Metal Detectors at Entrances to Aqsa Mosque Compound," *New York Times*, July 24, 2017.

[25] Barak Ravid, "Israel Responds to Erdoğan: Temple Mount Statements 'Unfounded and Distorted,'" *Haaretz*, July 25, 2017.

Turkish President Erdoğan['s] statements to his party's activists are wacky, unfounded, and distorted. It would be better for him to deal with the problems and difficulties of his country. The days of the Ottoman Empire are long gone. The capital of the Jewish people had been, is and will be Jerusalem. Unlike in past years, it is a city whose government is committed to security, liberty, religious freedom, and respect for the rights of all minorities. He who lives in a glass house shouldn't throw stones.[26]

As in other regional affairs, Turkey's involvement in the July 2017 Temple Mount crisis was problematic not only from Israel's point of view. Turkey was aligned in its position with Hamas, the Muslim Brotherhood, and Qatar; on the other side were Jordan, Egypt, and even the PA. Turkey's actions in Jerusalem are seen by regional players as undesirable neo-Ottoman attempts to challenge their leadership and importance in the Sunni world.[27]

Complex Regional Standing Could Block Turkish Mediation on the Palestinian Front
Turkey's problematic relationships with the traditional Sunni Arab leading countries—Egypt, Jordan, and Saudi Arabia—could block any Turkish attempt to play a key political role in the Israeli-Palestinian peace process, even a positive role. Turkey has previously served as a regional mediator (e.g., between Israel and Syria) and still seeks to mediate between Israel and the Palestinians,[28] as well as between rival Palestinian factions Fatah and Hamas.[29] Nevertheless, Egypt would likely block Turkish involvement in the internal Palestinian arena as well as in any peace process between Israel and the Palestinians, seeing Ankara's move as an attempt to challenge Cairo as a regional hegemon.

Turkey's ability to mediate between the PA and Hamas is hampered not only because of its tense relations with Egypt and Israel, but also because the PA has not always considered Erdoğan as a fair broker, given his ideological alignment with Hamas.[30] Nevertheless, ties between Turkey and the PA have been solid. The PA has an embassy in Ankara, and the ambassador, Faed K. A. Mustafa (previously Palestinian ambassador to Russia), is considered an important political figure. As mentioned earlier, Turkey has a diplomatic mission in East Jerusalem led by an ambassador. Turkey

---

[26] Ravid, 2017.

[27] Discussion with Turkey expert at the Israeli National Security Council, Jerusalem, January 24, 2017.

[28] In early January 2018. Turkish Foreign Minister Mevlut Cavusoglu said that the two-state solution was the only viable path for the Israeli-Palestinian conflict and that Turkey was ready to mediate the peace process between Israelis and Palestinians. Saeed Abdul Razek, "Turkey Ready to Mediate Between Palestinians, Israelis," *Asharq Al-Awsat*, January 7, 2018.

[29] Muhammed Ammash, "The Israel-Turkey Deal Could Benefit the Palestinians," *Israel Turkey Policy Dialogue Publication Series*, Global Political Trends Center, Istanbul Kultur University, and Mitvim, February 2017.

[30] Telephone interview with a former Palestinian official, April 28, 2017.

was very active in helping the PA push for recognition at the UN. Turkish projects, including industrial zones, currently exist in PA-controlled areas of the West Bank, and more are planned.[31] On August 28, 2017, when UN Secretary-General António Guterres visited the West Bank, Palestinian President Mahmoud Abbas canceled his meeting with him and instead went to Turkey to meet with Erdoğan. However, it was unclear whether the visit to Ankara indicated closer PA ties with Turkey or rather Abbas's dissatisfaction with both the UN and Egypt.[32] Nevertheless, improvement of ties between Ramallah and Ankara seems more plausible after Erdoğan became the key champion against the Jerusalem recognition; the PA's main allies (Saudi Arabia, Jordan, Egypt, and the UAE) were seen as only paying lip service by objecting to the announcement.

Some in Israel's diplomatic corps could see a possible future role for Turkey as a mediator between Israel and Hamas, but that is not something Israeli officials discuss publicly.[33] Reports about such an attempt surfaced in March 2017 when Turkish Foreign Minister Mevlut Cavusoglu during a meeting in Washington announced that his country "has pressured Hamas to shift away from armed resistance" and negotiate with Israel, and that Hamas showed willingness to recognize Israel. Hamas quickly denied this through an official statement dismissing the report and an anonymous Hamas source on an Iranian website denying caving into Turkish pressure on Israel.[34] The Iranian link is important, as it may indicate that Turkey's ability to bring Hamas closer to Israel's position is limited. Indeed, Turkey still shelters elements of Hamas's military wing, but its support for Hamas is more on the political side, which is losing power to the military wing. The key backer of the military wing is Iran, and as the military wing becomes stronger, so does Iran's ability to influence the movement at the expense of Turkey. The interplay between Tehran and Ankara on the Palestinian front is just one of many manifestations of their ongoing regional dynamic.[35]

Once Aligned, Israel and Turkey Prioritize Different Objectives in Syria

Israeli-Turkish mutual perception of Syria as a security threat was in large part the basis for the countries' strategic alliance in the 1990s. In the mid-2000s, Turkey enjoyed close ties with Assad and tried to mediate peace talks between Israel and Syria.[36] How-

---

[31] Telephone interview with a former Palestinian official, April 28, 2017.

[32] Pinhas Inbari, "Why Did the PA's Mahmoud Abbas Avoid the UN Secretary-General When He Toured the Region?" *Jerusalem Center for Public Affairs*, September 4, 2017.

[33] Telephone discussion with an Israeli diplomat, March 1, 2017.

[34] Adnan Abu Amer, "Is Turkey Trying to Bypass Abbas in Gaza?" *Al-Monitor*, March 30, 2017.

[35] Email exchange with an Israeli think tank expert on Turkey, January 19, 2018.

[36] Nasi, 2017.

ever, at the onset of the civil war in Syria, Turkey was seen as the leader in the battle to overthrow Assad. It even undertook substantial risks in confronting Russia, with the downing of Russia's bomber in 2015, after Moscow came to the rescue of the Assad regime.[37] Even if Israel did not push explicitly for ousting Assad, it did support Turkey's stance, if only to break a critical node of Iranian influence.[38]

Turkey and Israel, each for its own reasons, have shared an anxiety over Iran's hegemonic regional aspirations. Israel, like other Sunni Arab countries that are U.S. allies, has hoped to see Turkey as a check on the political and security threats posed by Iran, especially as those have become more acute since the overturning of the Sunni-led regime in Baghdad and the growth of Iranian influence in Iraq and Syria. Especially meaningful was Erdoğan's mid-2017 rebuke of "Persian nationalism," which indicated that Turkey has continued to adhere to the same positions.[39] In practice, however, Turkey has not always lived up to these aspirations. In the second half of 2017, in light of the imminent victory of Assad, it changed its position and stopped challenging Damascus and its backers.[40] As noted earlier, the Astana Process suggests that Turkey might concede its anti-Iranian demands—a prospect that worries Israel as well as Jordan, Egypt, Saudi Arabia, and the UAE.[41]

Longstanding Israeli Support for Kurdish Independence Causes Turkish Backlash

Israel has maintained discreet military, intelligence, and business ties with the Kurds since the 1960s, partially to create a buffer against common Arab adversaries (primarily Saddam Hussein's Iraq) and Iran. In June 2014, Netanyahu was the first world leader supporting the establishment of Kurdish independence in northern Iraq because

---

[37]   Gareth Porter, "The Real Reason for Turkey's Shoot-Down of the Russian Jet," *Middle East Eye*, November 30, 2015.

[38]   Israeli officials debated about the best policy vis-à-vis Syria. On the one hand, some analysts did not see the continuation of the Assad regime as necessarily a problem, as it was the "devil" Israel has known, but others advocated helping to oust the regime in the hope that a more favorable alternative would emerge. In the end, Israel did neither one, but throughout the war kept its redlines—preventing the transfer of advanced weapons to Hezbollah and the establishment of Iranian weapon factories in Syria (discussion with a former Israeli security official at the RAND Corporation, October 30, 2017).

[39]   "Erdoğan: Listu Radian 'an At-Tawasu' Al-Farasi, [Erdoğan: I Am Not Content with Persian Expansionism]," *Asharq al-Awsat*, June 17, 2017. Erdoğan has also used the phrase in the past, specifically to critique Iranian influence exerted through the Popular Mobilization Units in Iraq.

[40]   Mohamed Talib Hamid, *Al-Siyasa Al-Kharijiya Al-Turkiya wa Athriha 'ala Al-Amn Al-'Arabi* [Turkish Foreign Policy and Its Impact on Arab Security], Cairo: Al-Arabi Publishing, 2016.

[41]   Uzi Rabi and Chelsi Mueller, "The Gulf Arab States and Israel Since 1967: From 'No Negotiation' to Tacit Cooperation," *British Journal of Middle Eastern Studies*, Vol. 44, No. 4, 2017, pp. 576–592.

"they deserve it."[42] The same month, other Israeli officials echoed this support, including then–President Shimon Peres in a meeting with then–President Barack Obama, and then–Minister of Foreign Affairs Avigdor Lieberman with then–Secretary of State John Kerry.[43] In January 2016, Justice Minister Ayelet Shaked said that the "Kurdish people are a partner for the Israeli people."[44]

While earlier support for Iraqi Kurds was uncontroversial from Ankara's perspective, as it had increased cooperation with Erbil since 2007, circumstances changed in September 2017 because of the Kurdish referendum on independence.[45] That month, serving and former Israeli officials made several statements regarding the Kurds that were deemed problematic, not only in Turkey but also in the United States and Europe. Netanyahu, again, was the first world leader publicly supporting the referendum.[46] In addition, former deputy IDF chief of staff Major General Yair Golan, in his first U.S. public address since retiring, said that the PKK was in his view not a terrorist organization (the PKK is designated as a terrorist movement by Turkey, the European Union, and the United States). Netanyahu subsequently negated this statement, but he reiterated his support for Kurdish independence. He also connected the Kurdish issue to Israeli-Turkish tensions over Hamas by saying that "Israel objects to the PKK and considers it a terrorist organization, unlike Turkey, which supports a different terrorist organization: Hamas."[47]

While not a new Israeli policy, Israel's vocal support of the Kurdish independence bid in late 2017 proved to rely on wrong assumptions. When Israel realized that this stance was causing unease in Washington, which wanted the Kurds to backtrack on the referendum, Netanyahu asked his ministers to tone down their public statements.[48] The reaction to Israel's public support of Kurdish independence in Turkey was as expected—it provoked the spread of conspiracy theories, and media affiliated with Erdoğan reported that Kurdish groups signed a secret agreement with Israel to gain their independence by resettling Jews in the region.[49] Tension between Israel and Turkey escalated after Erdoğan accused the Mossad, Israel's clandestine intelligence agency, of standing behind the referendum.[50]

[42] Barak Ravid, "Netanyahu Calls for Kurdish Independence from Iraq," *Haaretz*, June 30, 2014.

[43] Dan Williams, "Israel Tells U.S. Kurdish Independence is 'Foregone Conclusion,'" Reuters, June 26, 2014.

[44] Tamar Pileggi, "Justice Minister Calls for an Independent Kurdistan," *Times of Israel*, January 20, 2016.

[45] Email exchange with a Turkey expert at an Israeli think tank, January 19, 2018.

[46] Jeffrey Heller, "Israel Endorses Independent Kurdish State," Reuters, September 13, 2017.

[47] Moran Azulay, "PM Refutes Fmr. Dep. IDF Chief's PKK Comments," *Ynet News*, September 12, 2017.

[48] "Netanyahu Orders Ministers to Keep Mum on Kurdish Referendum," *Times of Israel*, September 25, 2017.

[49] O'Connor, 2017.

[50] Ari Khalidi, "Meeting Rouhani, Erdogan Claims Mossad Behind Kurdistan Referendum," *Kurdistan 24*, October 9, 2017.

For Israel, Cyprus and Greece Play Turkey's Traditional Role

With the downturn in Israeli-Turkish relations in 2010, Israel substantially advanced its ties with Greece and Cyprus. While Greek-Turkish relations are on a positive track, renewal of ties with Turkey can risk Israel's relations with Cyprus, something that Israel is trying to avoid. Cyprus has historically viewed Israel suspiciously because Israel used to sell Turkey weapons that theoretically could be used against Cyprus.[51] Several factors changed this dynamic. The economic crisis in Greece, combined with the Arab Spring—which made Arab countries too preoccupied to pay attention to Cyprus—pushed Cyprus to look to find a new partner in Israel. From Israel's perspective, that was an important development; until then, when forced to pick sides, Israel would choose Turkey over Cyprus. In 2010, while Israel was estranged from Turkey, both Israel and Cyprus were open to deeper engagement.

Ties between Israel and Cyprus (and Greece) improved quickly on multiple levels—economically, diplomatically, and in terms of security engagement. As mentioned earlier, Cyprus's position on a possible passage of a gas pipeline between Israel and Turkey through its waters is one of the critical factors that could derail an Israeli-Turkish energy deal. Diplomatically, Cyprus and Greece help Israel deal with the European Union, a difficult political front.[52] Engagement with Greece and Cyprus filled a gap in Israel's regional strategy, and the IDF even conducted joint air and naval military exercises with both countries.[53]

Israeli officials always have said that relations with Cyprus would not come at the expense of other countries, and that ties with Cyprus would not be undermined by relations with other countries (i.e., Turkey). After reconciliation with Turkey, Israel is trying hard to keep its word and maintain strong relations with both Greece and Cyprus, even as it mends fences with Turkey.

Once the Bedrock of Ties, Security Cooperation Unlikely to Grow Soon

While defense ties were historically the bedrock of Israeli-Turkish relations, the prospect of cooperation on those issues in the post-normalization era is the most controversial. Under Lieberman, all defense deals with Turkey are blocked. The only exception is intelligence sharing pertaining to terrorism, which continued even during the six-year crisis between the two countries.[54]

---

[51] Telephone discussion with an Israeli diplomat, March 1, 2017.

[52] Telephone discussion with an Israeli diplomat, March 1, 2017.

[53] Discussion with Turkey expert at the Israeli National Security Council, Jerusalem, January 24, 2017.

[54] Interview with a former Israeli ambassador to Turkey, Jerusalem, January 24, 2017.

The reasons for the limited partnership are the same as those that hinder closer diplomatic cooperation. First, Israel is concerned over Turkey's ties with Hamas. According to an NSC staffer, the guiding principle for Israel should be that Turkey-Hamas ties need to cease completely before security cooperation resumes—and that, according to Israeli assessments, is unlikely to happen.[55]

In addition, given Turkey's softening stance toward the Assad regime, Iran, and Russia, Israeli-Turkish security cooperation—which in the past aimed at rolling back Iranian influence and achieving mutual regional objectives—is not viable in the near term. There is a specific risk related to Iran when it comes to defense cooperation. In 2013, a series of articles in the U.S. press accused Turkey of selling out Israel to Iran, delivering a blow to Israeli intelligence. Former Mossad head Danny Yatom was quoted saying that "We are suspicious of the Turks that they relay information to Iran that can endanger us."[56]

Moreover, Cyprus and Greece have taken over Turkey's traditional roles in joint naval and air exercises with Israel. Cyprus is anxious about Israel's rapprochement with Turkey, and not selling weapons to Turkey is one way of keeping Cyprus as a reliable ally.[57]

Finally, while Israelis, for the most part, do not see Turkey per se as a security risk, officials in the defense and diplomatic realms consider Erdoğan unreliable, erratic, and even anti-Semitic.[58] Many explicitly say that as long as Erdoğan is Turkey's leader, security partnership is out of the question.[59] That sentiment became stronger in light of Turkey's threats and actions that could again lead to the downgrading of ties with Israel.

While substantial improvement in security ties would require that Israel and Turkey come closer together on these different diplomatic dimensions, some Israeli-Turkish cooperation could emerge in the context of NATO. By removing its veto, Turkey enabled formal Israeli-NATO collaboration—a high priority for Israel. An important milestone was a meeting between Turkey's Chief of Staff General Hulusi Akar and IDF Deputy Chief of Staff Major General Yair Golan on the sidelines of a meeting of NATO military leaders in January 2017, the first such meeting since before the *Mavi Marmara* incident. Although the meeting was reportedly symbolic, its mere

---

[55] Discussion with Turkey expert at the Israeli National Security Council, Jerusalem, January 24, 2017; a Turkish journalist and scholar agreed with this assessment.

[56] Cengiz Çandar, "Turkey: The Self-Fulfilling Prophecy of the Hakan Fidan Story," *Al Monitor*, October 21, 2013.

[57] Telephone discussion with an Israeli diplomat, March 1, 2017.

[58] Interview with a former MFA official who served in Turkey, Jerusalem, January 24, 2017; Svante Cornell, "Erdogan's Turkey: The Role of a Little Known Islamist Poet," *Breaking Defense*, January 2, 2018.

[59] Discussion with Middle East experts at the Israeli National Security Council, Jerusalem, December 13, 2017.

existence was interpreted as a sign of warming security relations.[60] (Only some eight months later, Golan would say that he did not see the PKK as a terrorist organization.)[61]

Although official Israeli policy blocks weapon sales to Turkey, the defense industries in both countries have been eager to collaborate again.[62] In terms of training and weapon sales, Turkey is interested in specific Israeli capabilities—improving urban warfare[63]—and certain technologies, such as cyber, UAVs, and the Iron Dome missile defense system.[64] Although Israel has thus far refused these requests, if conditions improve, the strong defense lobby in Israel could pressure the Ministry of Defense to be more lenient in its Turkey policy.[65] An Israeli diplomat confirmed this assessment:

> Our formal policy is that we don't sell Turkey any weapon systems, even though it can be very lucrative for Israel. However, each case is examined separately. The defense industries in both countries very much want to go back to collaboration, but the Ministry of Defense now stops everything. It would be hard to sustain the pressure for a long time if there is no good reason to oppose collaboration. Depending on developments, it is possible that gradually companies will go back to doing business in the defense realm, beginning with cyber and turning to other things. Notwithstanding this pressure, though, Israel should be careful and not rush to Turkey's arms again, and so far, that's what we are careful [about].[66]

Conclusion

This chapter explored the key standing political issues between Israel and Turkey: the Palestinian issue (specifically, Gaza, the AKP's affiliation with Hamas, and Jerusalem); the diverging Israeli and Turkish approaches toward Iran in the aftermath of the Syrian civil war; and Israel's support for Kurdish independence and its strengthening ties with Cyprus. These differences, combined with complete lack of trust between the Israeli and Turkish governments, make diplomatic and security cooperation unlikely in the near future. The magnitude of these issues creates an unfavorable atmosphere that could also hinder the advancement of mutual economic interests.

---

[60] Herb Keinon, "Israeli, Turkish Generals Meet for First Time in Years," *Jerusalem Post*, January 19, 2017.

[61] Azulay, 2017.

[62] Discussion with Israeli MFA officials, Jerusalem, December 13, 2017.

[63] Telephone discussion with a Turkey expert at an Israeli think tank, January 25, 2017.

[64] Discussion with Israeli MFA officials, Jerusalem, December 13, 2017.

[65] Interview with an Israeli Turkey expert, Tel Aviv, January 25, 2017.

[66] Telephone discussion with an Israeli diplomat, March 1, 2017.

CHAPTER SIX

Conclusion: Israeli-Turkish Ties Face Formidable Challenges

This report has provided an overview of Israeli-Turkish relations as of January 2018. As previously demonstrated, ties between Israel and Turkey since the June 2016 rapprochement have been inconsistent. The first 11 months after the agreement were characterized almost solely by positive trends, mainly in economic areas but also in restoring and maintaining diplomatic ties; there were signs of initial military discussions, primarily about the topic of NATO. Since then, however, diplomatic tensions have arisen, reminding spectators that fundamental differences remain between these two former allies. In May 2018, after the IDF killed dozens of Palestinians and injured over 2,000 in violent protests in Gaza, Turkey expelled the Israeli ambassador, and Israel responded by expelling the Turkish consul from Jerusalem; the incidents were accompanied by public humiliation of diplomatic staff and a war of words between Turkish and Israeli politicians.[1] Even before, in multiple incidents, Erdoğan has lambasted Israel after the latter instituted controversial policies related to the Palestinians. Israel, which has traditionally avoided responding to Erdoğan to prevent escalation, has changed its policy and responded in kind. The Israeli government's objective in rebuking Erdoğan and other Turkish officials is demonstrating to Turkey that it would not bow its head indefinitely, hoping to stop the anti-Israel slurs. It is too early to say whether this strategy is achieving its goal, but so far it does not look as if it made Erdoğan lower his tone.

In their reprimands, Israeli politicians are aiming at Erdoğan personally, attacking his autocratic rule and treatment of minorities, primarily the Kurds. The personal nature of the response to Erdoğan is not coincidental. In Israeli eyes, the once multifaceted Turkey is now ruled completely by its autocratic, unreliable, possibly anti-Semitic president. The outcome of the April 16, 2017, referendum, which granted sweeping powers to Erdoğan, reaffirmed Israel's suspicions that his 15-year rule is going to be extended and become even more centralized, possibly extending divisions further.[2]

The main divisions between Israel and Turkey are on the political side, as discussed in Chapter Five. These include different priorities in Syria, affecting their

---

[1] Landau and Lis, 2018; Bachner et al., 2018.

[2] Email interview with an Israeli diplomat in Turkey, April 21, 2017.

respective approaches to Iran, and differences on the Kurdish issue. Moreover, deterioration of U.S.-Turkish ties in 2017 have put Israel and Turkey on opposing sides of the U.S. camp. Nonetheless, the main point of contention between the two countries has not changed in decades, and that is the Israeli-Palestinian conflict. Israeli-Turkish relations have always been sensitive to developments in the Arab-Israeli and the Israeli-Palestinian conflicts. While Turkey is far from the only country criticizing Israel's policies toward the Palestinians, and like other countries in the Muslim and Arab worlds it uses anti-Israel rhetoric to garner domestic and regional support, Turkey's behavior is abnormal for countries that enjoy positive relations with Israel. Moreover, Erdoğan's choice of words is seen in Israel as a reflection of his anti-Semitic beliefs.[3] His government is seen as legitimizing the spread of such views in Turkey through domestic media[4] and marginalizing the Jewish community in Turkey.[5] For that reason, Israel does not see Turkey as a reliable partner on sensitive matters "as long as Erdoğan is in charge."[6]

Still, Israel and Turkey have some strong mutual interests. In the economic arena, both countries stand to gain from more cooperation in trade, tourism, and energy. On the security and diplomatic front, both countries are interested in preventing a humanitarian crisis in Gaza. Further, while there are doubts regarding Turkey's commitment to an anti-Iran opposition in Syria, and suspicion that it instead favors the protection of its narrower anti-Kurdish interest,[7] in the long run, Turkey is opposed to expansion of Iranian influence in the Middle East.[8] Given its critical regional role as a large Sunni country, located strategically between Asia and Europe, with a highly educated population, Turkey might be too important to give up on completely.

Yet, while in the past Israel had almost no alternative to Turkey as an economic, diplomatic, or security partner in the region, the situation is different now. From the economic perspective, as explained in Chapter Four, countries such as Greece and Cyprus have substituted for Turkey as nearby affordable tourism destinations for large parts of the Jewish population (although tourism to Turkey among the Arab Israeli population has been on the rise). Further, although Israel and Turkey are still formally exploring the gas deal, Israel is examining other alternatives, such as the EastMed pipeline being negotiated with Cyprus, Greece, and Italy. In addition, while Turkey has been seeking to reduce its energy dependence on Russian gas, its late-2017 col-

---

3   Zvika Klein, "Biglal Ha'Antishemiyut: Yahadut Turkia Mechapeset Miklat," *Maariv*, March 21, 2015.

4   "Israel-Turkey Tensions High over TV Series," 2010.

5   Klein, 2015.

6   Interview with a former Israeli security official, Santa Monica, Calif., October 30, 2017.

7   Fehim Tastekin, "Turkey, Iran, Iraq in Shaky Alignment Against Iraqi Kurdistan," *Al-Monitor*, September 29, 2017.

8   "Erdoğan: Listu Radian 'an At-Tawasu' Al-Farasi, [Erdoğan: I Am Not Content with Persian Expansionism]," 2017.

laboration with Moscow in advancing the TurkStream gas pipeline from Russia to Turkey and the Akkuyu nuclear power plant project suggests that this has become less of a priority. Israel and Turkey have been historically effective at separating economics from politics, but the "poisonous" political atmosphere between the two countries adds political risks that investors and businesspeople may wish to avoid, possibly hampering progress on the economic front.[9]

Meanwhile, Israel has found substitutes for Turkey's diplomatic and security roles. Greece, Cyprus, and other countries have replaced Turkey in joint and combined military exercises after Turkish airspace was closed to IDF flights.[10] Moreover, whereas during the 1990s and most of the 2000s, Turkey was an important export market for the Israeli defense industries, other, larger markets are now available and offer lucrative opportunities, such as Japan, South Korea, and India (the latter of which is now Israel's leading arms buyer).[11] In addition, while Turkey was historically Israel's only Muslim-majority ally, Israel now enjoys backchannel relations with Saudi Arabia and the UAE.[12] Ties with Egypt and Jordan, with which Israel has peace agreements, have been steadily improving.[13] These countries all share Israel's concerns about Iran as well as the Muslim Brotherhood and Hamas, with which the AKP ideologically identifies.

All that does not mean that Israel and Turkey no longer share common interests. But if the 69-year-old record of bilateral ties teaches one lesson, it is that Israeli-Turkish relations in the near-to-medium-term will be linked to developments on the Israeli-Palestinian front. Presumably, if present trends continue, ties will remain the same—political and security relations will stay cold, while business sectors work to expand relations. Periodic outbursts related to the Palestinian issue are expected. Under this scenario, the relationship may not break down completely, although threats to cut ties and mutual expulsion of each other's envoys are certainly unhelpful.[14]

Israel and Turkey will continue to share common objectives and should find ways to agree on an approach to rehabilitate Gaza, once the dust settles over the May 2018 crisis. Both countries are interested in preventing a humanitarian disaster in Gaza, and

---

[9]   Email exchange with a Turkey expert at an Israeli think tank, January 19, 2018.

[10]   In 2010, it was leaked that the IDF was training in Romania after the worsening of relations with Turkey. Romania was selected specifically because some areas in the Carpathian Mountains are similar to some regions in Iran (Mihaela Iordache, "Israel Trains in Romania, Thinking About Teheran," *Osservatorio Balcani e Caucaso—Transeuropa*, August 11, 2010).

[11]   Amos Harel, "Israel's India Missile Deal Will Be Partially Implemented After Netanyahu's Attempts at Persuasion," *Haaretz*, January 21, 2018.

[12]   Clive Jones and Yoel Guzansky, "Israel's Relations with the Gulf States: Toward the Emergence of a Tacit Security Regime?" *Contemporary Security Policy*, Vol. 38, No. 3, 2017, pp. 398–419.

[13]   See, for example, Zena Tahhan, "Egypt-Israel Relations 'at Highest Level' in History," *Al Jazeera*, September 20, 2017.

[14]   "Turkish FM: No Danger to Israel-Turkey Relations," 2018.

Israel continues to welcome Turkey's reconstruction efforts.[15] One of the challenges for Israel is that Turkey's aid to Gaza is channeled through several governmental and nongovernmental organizations, including the İHH. In March 2017, Israel arrested the manager of the Gaza branch of the governmental organization Turkish International Cooperation and Development Agency (TIKA) on suspicion that he funneled aid money to Hamas's military wing. This operative was also linked to İHH.[16] The Turkish MFA expressed solidarity with the TIKA worker, risking possible escalation between Turkey and Israel.[17] Nevertheless, despite warnings that this incident demonstrates the strong Turkey-Hamas military ties, the Israeli government asserted that Turkey was not aware of the manager's actions and that Hamas took advantage of Turkey's generosity.[18] Such developments are expected to emerge in time, and the way the Turkish and Israeli governments decide to handle them will determine to what extent tensions will rise.

The June 2017 crisis over Temple Mount was also an example of possible mitigation approaches that Turkey and Israel might adopt. Following their mutual recriminations over the holy site, Erdoğan requested to speak with Rivlin instead of Netanyahu. Rivlin took the call despite MFA objections[19] and political rhetoric that suggested that Israel should retaliate with a review of relations with Turkey, recognition of an independent Kurdistan, and acknowledgment of the Armenian genocide.[20] This telephone conversation illustrated how Israel and Turkey can maintain diplomatic ties even during the height of a crisis.

A substantial change, for good or bad, in the Israeli-Palestinian arena could shift Israeli-Turkish relations in one of two directions. Analysts consider another war in Gaza to be only a matter of time.[21] From Israel's perspective, bilateral relations could withstand such a war as long as Turkey separates its strong ideological and practical ties with Hamas and support for the Palestinians from its pragmatic bilateral ties with Israel. This may not be that simple. Israelis in the defense realm feared that escalation

---

[15]   Avi Issacharoff, "Hamas Says Turkey to Send Fuel to End Gaza Electricity Crisis," *Times of Israel*, January 14, 2017.

[16]   Yonah Jeremy Bob, "Israel Arrests Head of Turkish Humanitarian Group in Gaza for Financing Hamas," *Jerusalem Post*, March 21, 2017.

[17]   "Turkish Foreign Ministry Voices Solidarity with TIKA Worker Arrested by Israel," *Hurriyet Daily News*, March 22, 2017.

[18]   Avi Issacharof, "Arrest of Gaza Manager Exposes Hamas's Turkish Connection," *Times of Israel*, March 21, 2017; Bob, 2017.

[19]   Ravid, 2017.

[20]   Raphael Ahren, "Lapid Calls for More Aggressive Stance on Turkey," *Times of Israel*, July 27, 2017. Threats to recognize the Armenian genocide resurfaced in May 2018, after the diplomatic feud between Turkey and Israel over the death toll in Gaza and the move of the U.S. embassy to Jerusalem.

[21]   Amos Harel, "Gaza Power Crisis Explained: Why Israel and Hamas Are Heading for a Face-Off Neither Side Wants," *Haaretz*, June 12, 2017.

in the Israeli-Palestinian conflict, be it another round of fighting in Gaza, a third intifada, or Israeli annexation of parts of the West Bank (as proposed by certain members of government) would make Turkey withdraw its ambassador and freeze ties again;[22] their prediction materialized in May 2018. At the time of writing, it is unclear whether this estrangement is permanent; however, it is evident that negative developments on the Palestinian front will continue to pose formidable obstacles to Israeli-Turkish ties.

Alternatively, it is safe to assume that a meaningful breakthrough in the Israeli-Palestinian peace process would lead to changes in Turkey's approach toward Israel and help bring the two countries closer together. As with the Madrid peace conference in 1991, the Oslo Accords and Israel's disengagement from Gaza, Turkey is likely to respond positively to progress on the Palestinian front and strengthen its ties with Israel. Further, having sought a mediator role in the past, Turkey is still interested in mediating talks between Israelis and Palestinians and helping to advance a two-state solution to the conflict.[23]

Absent a meaningful development on the Israeli-Palestinian front, or substantial political changes in Israel, Turkey, or the region—none of which seem likely in the near future—Israel and Turkey need to be more motivated to sustain and better relations. Although the anti-Israeli rhetoric has become a standard operating procedure on Erdoğan's part, this is not something Israelis are willing to get used to. Its rebukes of Erdoğan in return, however, may not be the most effective way of stopping the invective. Despite lower incentives for cooperation, seven decades of bilateral relations have shown that when Israel and Turkey want to collaborate, they find ways to do so, despite divisions.

Israeli-Turkish Ties Have Important Implications for the United States

The United States was pivotal for achieving Israeli-Turkish reconciliation. After the Obama administration attempted, unsuccessfully, to prevent the downgrading of diplomatic ties, it facilitated confidence-building measures during the crisis years.[24] In 2013, it worked diligently with both sides to arrange an apology by Netanyahu to Erdoğan.[25] What could explain U.S. efforts at the time to mediate between Israel and Turkey? Clearly, the nature of Israeli-Turkish relations has traditionally had several implications for the United States. First, good Israeli-Turkish relations have enabled a trilateral strategic U.S.-Israel-Turkey conversation to enhance regional stability (or at

---

[22] Peter Beaumont, "Far-Right Israeli Minister Plans Bill to Annex One of Biggest Settlements," *The Guardian*, January 3, 2017.

[23] "Turkish FM: No Danger to Israel-Turkey Relations," 2018.

[24] Arbel, 2014; Pfeffer, 2013.

[25] Arbel, 2014.

the very least not add an additional difficult component to a complicated region) and promote shared economic interests. The three countries have traditionally had mutual interests vis-à-vis Iran, Syria, and fighting terrorism. Israel's new association with NATO could be another avenue for U.S.-Turkish-Israeli cooperation, which is in the United States' interest and hinges on continued Turkish consent. The first U.S. permanent military base in Israel, an air defense facility established in September 2017 under the U.S. European Command, is another indication of the importance the United States attributes to security ties with Israel in the context of the Middle East, Europe, and, by extension, NATO.[26]

The United States also has geostrategic and economic interests in a possible Israeli-Turkish-Cypriot gas deal. From a U.S. perspective, a NATO member (Turkey), a European Union partner (Cyprus), and an important ally (Israel) could be the beneficiaries of Mediterranean gas discoveries at the expense of Russia and Iran. Economically, Texas-based Noble Energy Inc. is the second largest partner in the Leviathan gas field, with holdings of 39.7 percent.[27] Moreover, despite notable challenges, Turkey's ties with Hamas could be helpful as the United States and the international community seek to promote an Israeli-Palestinian peace process.

Although these interests are enduring, relations between the United States and Turkey have deteriorated since the attempted military coup against Erdoğan in mid-2016 and the U.S. refusal to extradite self-exiled Turkish cleric Fethullah Gülen, whom Erdoğan blames for the coup.[28]

While Turkey has traditionally played a balancing game, maintaining close ties with the United States and NATO as well as varying degrees of cooperation with Iran, Syria, and Russia, recent developments suggest that the balancing act has become less delicate. The severe Turkish response to the U.S. recognition of Jerusalem as Israel's capital, essentially leading the protest against the move, and the withdrawal of its ambassador to the United States after the opening of the embassy in Jerusalem suggest possible further deterioration of U.S.-Turkish ties.

In the long run, however, the United States also sees Turkey as an important regional player—large, populous, technologically advanced, and militarily capable—that can contribute to the Sunni balance against Iran. Better Israeli-Turkish ties in this context would be important for advancing regional stability and rallying a regional coalition that includes both countries to roll back Iranian influence. While Turkey's ties with both the United States and Israel were at a low point as of January 2018, the

---

[26] Judah Ari Gross, "In First, U.S. Establishes Permanent Military Base in Israel," *Times of Israel*, September 18, 2017.

[27] Yaacov Benmeleh and David Wainer, "Israel and Turkey Seek to Shield Natural Gas Ties from Politics," *Bloomberg*, December 12, 2016.

[28] This also directly affects Israel-Turkey relations, as the coup is seen as a Gülen-U.S.-Zionist conspiracy (Tzou, 2017).

United States still has strong leverage over Israel and Turkey and can use it to continue facilitating positive interactions between the two sides on multiple levels. If it chooses to do so, the U.S. government can push the two sides to separate their ideological differences from their pragmatic ties and to avoid escalatory rhetoric on sensitive issues—be it the Temple Mount or Kurdish independence. In addition, the United States can help shape Israeli-Turkish relations in the long term by pursuing a serious Israeli-Palestinian peace process. If history is an indication, improvement in Israeli-Palestinian relations will be followed by improvement in Israeli-Turkish relations.

References

Abdel Kader, Mohammad, "Turkey's Relationship with the Muslim Brotherhood," *Al Arabiya Institute for Studies*, October 14, 2013. As of March 30, 2017:
http://english.alarabiya.net/en/perspective/alarabiya-studies/2013/10/14/Turkey-s-relationship-with-the-Muslim-Brotherhood.html

Abdul Razek, Saeed, "Turkey Ready to Mediate Between Palestinians, Israelis," *Asharq Al-Awsat*, January 7, 2018. As of January 7, 2018:
https://aawsat.com/english/home/article/1135811/turkey-ready-mediate-between-palestinians-israelis

Abu Amer, Adnan, "Is Turkey Trying to Bypass Abbas in Gaza?" *Al-Monitor*, March 30, 2017. As of March 30, 2017:
http://www.al-monitor.com/pulse/originals/2017/03/turkey-hamas-pressure-peace-process-israel.html

Ahren, Raphael, "In Battle for the Skies, Turkey Beats Israel 112:0," *Times of Israel*, October 31, 2013. As of March 30, 2017:
https://www.timesofisrael.com/in-battle-for-the-skies-turkey-beats-israel-1120

———, "Lapid Calls for More Aggressive Stance on Turkey," *Times of Israel*, July 27, 2017. As of July 27, 2017:
https://www.timesofisrael.com/lapid-calls-for-more-aggressive-stance-on-turkey

———, "Israel Expels Turkish Consul in Jerusalem After Ankara Boots Israel's Ambassador," *Times of Israel*, May 15, 2018. As of May 16, 2018:
https://www.timesofisrael.com/israel-expels-turkish-consul-in-jerusalem-as-gaza-spat-intensifies/

"All You Need to Know About the Israel-Turkey Reconciliation," *Haaretz*, June 27, 2016. As of March 30, 2017:
http://www.haaretz.com/israel-news/1.727208

Alon, Amir, "Turkish Ambassador to Israel Trying to Coax Israelis Back to Antalya," *Ynet News*, May 25, 2017. As of May 25, 2017:
https://www.ynetnews.com/articles/0,7340,L-4967500,00.html

Altunısık, Meliha, "The Turkish-Israeli Rapprochement in the Post–Cold War Era," *Middle Eastern Studies*, Vol. 36, No. 2, 2000, pp. 172–191.

Ammash, Muhammed, "The Israel-Turkey Deal Could Benefit the Palestinians," *Israel Turkey Policy Dialogue Publication Series*, Global Political Trends Center, Istanbul Kultur University, and Mitvim, February 2017. As of March 30, 2017:
http://gpotcenter.org/dosyalar/GPoT_Mitvim_Series_M.Ammash.pdf

Arbel, Dan, "The U.S.-Turkey-Israel Triangle," Washington, D.C.: Brookings Institution, Analysis Paper Number 34, October 2014. As of March 30, 2017:
https://www.brookings.edu/wp-content/uploads/2016/06/USTurkeyIsrael-TriangleFINAL.pdf

Aykan, Mahmut Bali, "The Turkey-U.S.-Israel Triangle: Continuity, Change, and Implications for Turkey's Post–Cold War Middle East Policy," *Journal of South Asian and Middle Eastern Studies*, Vol. 22, No. 4, Summer 1999.

Aytürk, İlker, "The Coming of an Ice Age? Turkish–Israeli Relations Since 2002," *Turkish Studies*, Vol. 12, No. 4, 2011, pp. 675–687.

Azulay, Moran, "PM Refutes Fmr. Dep. IDF Chief's PKK Comments," *Ynet*, September 12, 2017. As of September 12, 2017:
https://www.ynetnews.com/articles/0,7340,L-5015867,00.html

Azulay, Yuval, "Machon Ha'Yetzu: Ha'Piyus Im Turkkya Yiten 'Boost' Nosaf Le'Kishrey Ha'Sachar," *Globes*, June 27, 2016. As of March 16, 2018:
https://www.globes.co.il/news/article.aspx?did=1001135346

Bachner, Michael, and *Times of Israel* staff, "Turkey, Israel Humiliate Each Others' Envoys in Escalating Diplomatic Tiff," *Times of Israel*, May 16, 2018. As of May 18, 2018:
https://www.timesofisrael.com/expelled-israeli-ambassador-to-turkey-humiliated-at-airport/

Beaumont, Peter, "Far-Right Israeli Minister Plans Bill to Annex One of Biggest Settlements," *The Guardian*, January 3, 2017. As of March 30, 2017:
https://www.theguardian.com/world/2017/jan/03/
far-right-israel-minister-naftali-bennett-bill-annex-maale-adumim-settlement-palestinian-territories

Bengio, Ofra, *Turkish-Israeli Relationship: Changing Ties of the Middle Eastern Outsiders*, London: Palgrave Macmillan, 2004.

Benmeleh, Yaacov, "Spain's Union Fenosa Said Mulling Higher Israel Gas Imports," *Bloomberg News*, August 29, 2016. As of March 30, 2017:
https://www.bloomberg.com/news/articles/2016-08-29/
spain-s-union-fenosa-said-in-talks-to-boost-israel-gas-imports

Benmeleh, Yaacov, and David Wainer, "Israel and Turkey Seek to Shield Natural Gas Ties From Politics," *Bloomberg*, December 12, 2016. As of March 30, 2017:
https://www.bloomberg.com/news/articles/2016-12-12/
israel-and-turkey-seek-to-shield-natural-gas-ties-from-politics

Bennhold, Katrin, "Leaders of Turkey and Israel Clash at Davos Panel," *New York Times*, January 29, 2009. As of March 30, 2017:
http://www.nytimes.com/2009/01/30/world/europe/30clash.html?_r=0

Ben Tzion, Shira, Twitter post, 1:24 AM, July 12, 2017. As of April 12, 2018:
https://twitter.com/ShiraBenTzion/status/885052295326695424

Borger, Julian, "Turkey Confirms It Barred Israel from Military Exercise Because of Gaza War," *The Guardian*, October 12, 2009. As of March 30, 2017:
https://www.theguardian.com/world/2009/oct/12/turkey-israel-military-gaza

Cagaptay, Soner, "Turkey and U.S. Enter Most Important Crisis in Recent Memory," *Cipher Brief*, October 1, 2017. As of October 1, 2017:
https://www.thecipherbrief.com/article/middle-east/turkey-u-s-enter-important-crisis-recent-memory

Çandar, Cengiz, "Turkey: The Self-Fulfilling Prophecy of the Hakan Fidan Story," *Al-Monitor*, October 21, 2013. As of March 30, 2017:
http://www.al-monitor.com/pulse/originals/2013/10/hakan-fidan-turkey-politics-erdogan.html#ixzz55YQlf9E5

Çelikkol, Oğuz, *Turkish-Israeli Relations: Crises and Cooperation*, Israel Turkey Policy Dialogue Publication Series, Global Political Trends Center, Istanbul Kultur University, and Mitvim, November 2016. As of March 30, 2017:
http://gpotcenter.org/dosyalar/GPoT_Mitvim_Series_O.Celikkol.pdf

Cohen, Hedy, "Eni's Egypt Gas Find Limits Israel's Gas Export Options," *Globes*, September 1, 2015. As of April 12, 2018:
http://www.globes.co.il/en/article-enis-egypt-gas-find-limits-israels-export-options-1001065749

———, "Egypt's Zohr Gas Reservoir Estimate Keeps Growing," *Globes*, July 25, 2016. As of April 12, 2018:
http://www.globes.co.il/en/article-egypts-zohr-gas-reservoir-estimate-keeps-growing-1001141772

Cohen, Raphael S., David E. Johnson, David E. Thaler, Brenna Allen, Elizabeth M. Bartels, James Cahill, and Shira Efron, *Lessons from Israel's Wars in Gaza*, Santa Monica, Calif.: RAND Corporation, 2017. As of June 1, 2017:
https://www.rand.org/pubs/research_briefs/RB9975.html

Cohen, Tova, and Ari Rabinovitch, "Leviathan Gas Field Developers Approve $3.75 Billion Investment," Reuters, February 23, 2017. As of March 30, 2017:
http://www.reuters.com/article/us-israel-natgas-leviathan-idUSKBN1620OS

Cornell, Svante, "Erdogan's Turkey: The Role of a Little Known Islamist Poet," *Breaking Defense*, January 2, 2018. As of January 2, 2018:
https://breakingdefense.com/2018/01/erdogans-turkey-the-role-of-a-little-known-islamist-poet

Davidovich, Joshua, "Rebuffing Former Top General, Netanyahu Says Kurdish PKK a Terror Group," *Times of Israel*, September 13, 2017. As of September 13, 2017:
https://www.timesofisrael.com/rebuffing-former-top-general-netanyahu-says-kurdish-pkk-a-terror-group

Eichner, Itamar, "Israel Issues Travel Warning for Turkey, Jordan and Egypt," *Ynet News*, March 27, 2017. As of March 30, 2017:
http://www.ynetnews.com/home/0,7340,L-3082,00.html

Eisenbud, Daniel K., "Turkey Remains Popular Tourist Destination for Israeli Arabs," *Jerusalem Post*, January 1, 2017. As of March 30, 2017:
http://www.jpost.com/Business-and-Innovation/
Turkey-remains-popular-tourist-destination-for-Israeli-Arabs-477183

Elron, Efrat, *Antisemitism and Anti-Zionism in Turkey: From Ottoman Rule to AKP*, London: Routledge, 2017.

Eran, Oded, Elai Rettig, and Ofir Winter, "The Gas Deal with Egypt: Israel Deepens Its Anchor in the Eastern Mediterranean," INSS Insight No. 1033, March 12, 2018. As of March 16, 2018:
http://www.inss.org.il/publication/gas-deal-egypt-israel-deepens-anchor-eastern-mediterranean

"Erdogan: Israel a 'Terrorist State' that Kills Children," *Times of Israel*, December 10, 2017. As of December 10, 2017:
https://www.timesofisrael.com/turkish-leader-israel-a-terrorist-state-that-kills-children

"Erdoğan: Listu Radian 'an At-Tawasu' Al-Farasi, [Erdoğan: I Am Not Content with Persian Expansionism]," *Asharq al-Awsat*, June 17, 2017.

"Erdogan Says Turkey Aims to Open Embassy in East Jerusalem," Reuters, December 17, 2017. As of December 17, 2017:
https://www.reuters.com/article/us-usa-trump-israel-turkey/
erdogan-says-turkey-aims-to-open-embassy-in-east-jerusalem-idUSKBN1EB0H7

Gabai, Ramzi, "Lenatzel et Hamomentum Hachiyuvi," *Marker Magazine*, March 1, 2017. As of March 30, 2017:
http://www.export.gov.il/files/press/turkey2themarker010317.pdf?redirect=no

Greenberg, Joel, and Scott Wilson, "Obama Ends Israel Visit by Brokering End to Dispute with Turkey," *Washington Post*, March 22, 2013. As of March 30, 2017:
https://www.washingtonpost.com/world/middle_east/obama-ends-israel-visit-by-honoring-historic-figures/2013/03/22/7a489fc4-92e9-11e2-ba5b-550c7abf6384_story.html?utm_term=.163c0b3f635f

Gross, Judah Ari, "In First, U.S. Establishes Permanent Military Base in Israel," *Times of Israel*, September 18, 2017. As of September 18, 2017:
https://www.timesofisrael.com/in-first-us-establishes-permanent-military-base-in-israel/?utm_source=Sailthru&utm_medium=email&utm_campaign=New%20
Campaign&utm_term=%2ASituation%20Report

Hacaoglu, Selcan, "Turkey Lobbying Israel to Push Cyprus on Approving Gas Pipeline," *Bloomberg*, July 20, 2017. As of July 20, 2017:
https://www.bloomberg.com/news/articles/2017-07-20/
turkey-lobbying-israel-to-push-cyprus-on-approving-gas-pipeline

Harel, Amos, "Gaza Power Crisis Explained: Why Israel and Hamas Are Heading for a Face-off Neither Side Wants," *Haaretz*, June 12, 2017. As of June 12, 2017:
http://www.haaretz.com/israel-news/.premium-1.795201

———, "No One Wants a War in Gaza, but the First Israeli Casualty Could Change Everything," *Haaretz*, January 5, 2018. As of January 5, 2018:
https://www.haaretz.com/israel-news/.premium-no-one-wants-a-war-in-gaza-but-the-first-israeli-casualty-could-change-everything-1.5729411

———, "Israel's India Missile Deal Will Be Partially Implemented After Netanyahu's Attempts at Persuasion," *Haaretz*, January 21, 2018. As of January 21, 2018:
https://www.haaretz.com/israel-news/.premium-india-missile-deal-reflects-brave-new-world-of-arms-sales-1.5749777

Harvey, Benjamin, "Erdogan Says He'd Cut Israel Ties If Trump Acts on Jerusalem," *Bloomberg*, December 5, 2017. As of December 5, 2017:
https://www.bloomberg.com/news/articles/2017-12-05/
erdogan-threatens-to-cut-israel-ties-if-trump-moves-on-jerusalem

Hazou, Elias, "Reported Plans to Purchase Naval Gunships," *Cyprus Mail*, November 10, 2015. As of March 30, 2017:
http://cyprus-mail.com/2015/11/10/reported-plans-to-purchase-naval-gunships

———, "'Tripartite' Gas Would Be Double the Price, Experts Say," *Cyprus Mail*, February 7, 2016. As of March 30, 2017:
http://cyprus-mail.com/2016/02/07/tripartite-gas-would-be-double-the-price-experts-say

Heller, Jeffrey, "Israel Endorses Independent Kurdish State," Reuters, September 13, 2017. As of September 13, 2017:
https://www.reuters.com/article/us-mideast-crisis-kurds-israel/
israel-endorses-independent-kurdish-state-idUSKCN1BO0QZ

Henderson, Simon, "A Hamas Rocket Hitting Israeli Gas Platforms Could Re-Escalate the Gaza War," *Business Insider*, August 21, 2014. As of March 30, 2017:
http://www.businessinsider.com/rocket-hitting-gas-platforms-could-re-escalate-gaza-war-2014-8

Inbari, Pinhas, "Why Did the PA's Mahmoud Abbas Avoid the UN Secretary-General When He Toured the Region?" *Jerusalem Center for Public Affairs*, September 4, 2017. As of September 4, 2017: http://jcpa.org/pas-mahmoud-abbas-avoid-un-secretary-general-toured-region

Iordache, Mihaela, "Israel Trains in Romania, Thinking About Teheran," *Osservatorio Balcani e Caucaso—Transeuropa*, August 11, 2010. As of January 10, 2018: https://www.balcanicaucaso.org/eng/Areas/Romania/Israel-trains-in-Romania-thinking-about-Teheran-79216

"Israel and Turkey Normalization Deal Signed," *Globes*, June 28, 2016. As of March 30, 2017: http://www.globes.co.il/en/article-israel-turkey-normalization-deal-to-be-declared-today-1001135131

"Israel Consortium Signs 'Historic' 15-Year, $10b Gas Deal with Jordan," *Times of Israel*, September 26, 2016. As of March 30, 2017: http://www.timesofisrael.com/israel-consortium-signs-15-year-10b-gas-deal-with-jordan

"Israel Expects Gas to Flow from East Mediterranean to Europe," Associated Press, December 5, 2017. As of December 5, 2017: http://www.dailymail.co.uk/wires/ap/article-5147441/Israel-expects-gas-flow-east-Mediterranean-Europe.html

"Israel Has Deployed Its Iron Dome Missile-Defense System on Ships for First Time," Associated Press, November 28, 2017. As of November 28, 2017: http://www.businessinsider.com/ap-israels-iron-dome-system-deployed-on-ships-for-first-time-2017-11

"Israeli Tourists Flock to Turkey as Relations Normalize, Number of Tourists Rise 80 Percent," *Daily Sabah* and *Anadolu Agency*, February 5, 2017. As of March 30, 2017: https://www.dailysabah.com/tourism/2017/02/05/israeli-tourists-flock-to-turkey-as-relations-normalize-number-of-tourists-rise-80-percent

"Israel-Turkey Gas Pipeline Could Be Ready in Four Years—Company," Reuters, March 2, 2017. As of March 30, 2017: http://www.reuters.com/article/israel-energy-idUSL5N1GF3ZO

"Israel-Turkey Tensions High over TV Series," *CNN*, January 12, 2010. As of March 30, 2017: http://www.cnn.com/2010/WORLD/meast/01/12/turkey.israel

Issacharoff, Avi, "Hamas Says Turkey to Send Fuel to End Gaza Electricity Crisis," *Times of Israel*, January 14, 2017. As of March 30, 2017: http://www.timesofisrael.com/hamas-says-turkey-to-send-fuel-to-end-gaza-electricity-crisis

———, "Arrest of Gaza Manager Exposes Hamas's Turkish Connection," *Times of Israel*, March 21, 2017. As of March 30, 2017: http://www.timesofisrael.com/arrest-exposes-hamas-turkish-connection

Jeremy Bob, Yonah, "Israel Arrests Head of Turkish Humanitarian Group in Gaza for Financing Hamas," *Jerusalem Post*, March 21, 2017. As of March 30, 2017: http://www.jpost.com/Arab-Israeli-Conflict/Head-of-Turkish-aid-group-in-Gaza-arrested-by-Israel-funneled-humanitarian-funds-to-Hamas-484771

Jones, Clive, and Yoel Guzansky, "Israel's Relations with the Gulf States: Toward the Emergence of a Tacit Security Regime?" *Contemporary Security Policy*, Vol. 38, No. 3, 2017, pp. 398–419.

Jones, Dorian, "Turkey Hosts Iranian, Russian FMs as Ankara-NATO Dispute Festers," *Voice of America*, November 19, 2017. As of November 19, 2017: https://www.voanews.com/a/turkey-hosts-iranian-russian-foreign-ministers-nato/4125307.html

————, "Turkey Summit Blasts Trump Decision on Jerusalem," *Voice of America*, December 13, 2017. As of December 13, 2017:
https://www.voanews.com/a/islamic-world-meeting-regarding-trump-jerusalem-choice/4161688.html

Jörum, Emma Lundgren, *Beyond Syria's Borders: A History of Territorial Disputes in the Middle East*, London: IB Tauris, 2014.

Kambas, Michele, "Cyprus Blocks Israel-Turkey Gas Pipeline Until Ankara Mends Ties," *Haaretz*, July 6, 2016. As of March 30, 2017:
http://www.haaretz.com/israel-news/business/1.729122

Kanat, Kilic Bugra, "Turkish-Israeli Reset: Business As Usual?" *Middle East Policy Council*, Vol. 20, No. 2, Summer 2013. As of April 12, 2018:
http://www.mepc.org/journal/middle-east-policy-archives/turkish-israeli-reset-business-usual?print

Keinon, Herb, "Netanyahu Apologizes to Turkey over Gaza Flotilla," *Jerusalem Post*, March 22, 2013. As of March 30, 2017:
http://www.jpost.com/International/Obama-Netanyahu-Erdogan-speak-by-phone-307423

————, "Israel to Open Permanent Office at NATO HQ Five Years After Turkey Blocked Move," *Jerusalem Post*, May 4, 2016. As of March 16, 2018:
www.jpost.com/Israel-News/Israel-to-open-permanent-office-at-NATO-HQ-five-years-after-Turkey-blocked-move-453049

————, "Israeli, Turkish Generals Meet for First Time in Years," *Jerusalem Post*, January 19, 2017. As of March 30, 2017:
http://www.jpost.com/Israel-News/Politics-And-Diplomacy/Israeli-Turkish-generals-meet-for-first-time-in-years-478887

————, "Netanyahu Says Israel Will Not Be Lectured to by the Likes of Erdoğan," *Jerusalem Post*, December 10, 2017. As of December 10, 2017:
http://www.jpost.com/Arab-Israeli-Conflict/Netanyahu-says-Israel-will-not-be-lectured-to-by-the-likes-of-Erdogan-517620

Kershner, Isabel, "Israel Agrees to Remove Metal Detectors at Entrances to Aqsa Mosque Compound," *New York Times*, July 24, 2017. As of July 24, 2017:
https://www.nytimes.com/2017/07/24/world/middleeast/israel-jordan-aqsa-temple-mount-violence.html

Khalidi, Ari, "Meeting Rouhani, Erdogan Claims Mossad Behind Kurdistan Referendum," *Kurdistan 24*, October 4, 2017. As of October 4, 2017:
http://www.kurdistan24.net/en/news/52ec5b3c-9967-4c24-a161-a6f5babf7069

Klein, Zvika, "Biglal Ha'Antishemiyut: Yahadut Turkia Mechapeset Miklat," *Maariv*, March 21, 2015. As of January 10, 2018:
https://www.makorrishon.co.il/nrg/online/1/ART2/684/812.html

Koren, David, and Ben Avrahami, "The Residents of Eastern Jerusalem at a Historic Crossroads," *Ha'Shiloach*, July 30, 2017. As of July 30, 2017:
https://hashiloach.org.il/residents-eastern-jerusalem-historic-crossroads

Landau, Noa, and Jonathan Lis, "Turkey and Israel Expel Envoys over Gaza Deaths," *Haaretz*, May 16, 2018. As of May 16, 2018:
https://www.haaretz.com/israel-news/turkey-expels-israel-s-ambassador-due-to-gaza-death-toll-1.6092965

Lehman, Eyaland, and Roi Kais, "Erdoğan Rebukes Israel over Muezzin Bill and Calls on Muslims to Go En Masse to Al-Aqsa," *Ynet News*, May 8, 2017. As of April 12, 2018:
https://www.ynetnews.com/articles/0,7340,L-4959239,00.html

Liel, Alon, "Turkey and Israel: A Chronicle of Bilateral Relations," Israel-Turkey Policy Dialogue Publication Series, Global Political Trends Center, Istanbul Kultur University, and Mitvim, February 2017. As of May 3, 2018:
http://mitvim.org.il/images/Alon_Liel_-_Turkey_and_Israel_-_A_Chronicle_of_Bilateral_Relations_-_February_2017.pdf

Lindenstrauss, Gallia, "Operation Protective Edge: Deepening the Rift Between Israel and Turkey," in Anat Kurz and Shlomo Brom, eds., *The Lessons of Operation Protective Edge*, Institute for National Security Studies, 2014. As of January 10, 2018:
http://www.inss.org.il/wp-content/uploads/systemfiles/Operation%20Protective%20Edge_%20Deepening%20the%20Rift%20between%20Israel%20and%20Turkey.pdf

"Mavi Marmara: Why Did Israel Stop the Gaza Flotilla?" *BBC News*, June 27, 2016. As of March 30, 2017:
http://www.bbc.com/news/10203726

Mitchell, Gabriel, "The Risks and Rewards of Israeli-Turkish Energy Cooperation," Israel Turkey Policy Dialogue Publication Series, Global Political Trends Center, Istanbul Kultur University, and Mitvim, January 2017. As of March 30, 2017:
http://gpotcenter.org/dosyalar/GPoT_Mitvim_Series_G.Mitchell.pdf

Moubayed, Sami, "Israel and Turkey Are Drifting Apart," *Gulf News*, January 19, 2010. As of March 30, 2017:
http://m.gulfnews.com/opinion/analysis/israel-and-turkey-are-drifting-apart-1.569958

Nasi, Selin, "Turkey-Israel Deal: A Key to Long-Term Reconciliation?" Israel Turkey Policy Dialogue Publication Series, Global Political Trends Center, Istanbul Kultur University, and Mitvim, January 2017. As of March 30, 2017:
http://mitvim.org.il/images/Selin_Nasi_-_The_Turkish-Israeli_Deal_-_Key_to_long-term_reconciliation_-_January_2017.pdf

Nelson, Zalman, "Did Israel Sign a Deal with Turkey to Import Water?" *Arutz Sheva*, July 7, 2009. As of March 30, 2017:
http://www.israelnationalnews.com/News/News.aspx/132267

"Netanyahu Orders Ministers to Keep Mum on Kurdish Referendum," *Times of Israel*, September 25, 2017. As of September 25, 2017:
https://www.timesofisrael.com/netanyahu-orders-ministers-to-keep-mum-on-kurdish-referendum/

O'Connor, Tom, "Turkey Tries to Scare Voters with Warning About Jews Ahead of Kurdish Referendum," *Newsweek*, September 15, 2017. As of September 15, 2017:
http://www.newsweek.com/turkey-fake-news-jews-promote-hate-kurds-iraq-666130

Palmer, Geoffrey, Alvaro Uribe, Joseph Ciechanover Itzhar, and Süleyman Özdem Sanberk, "Report of the Secretary-General's Panel of Inquiry on the 31 May 2010 Flotilla Incident," New York: United Nations, September 2, 2011. As of February 28, 2017:
http://www.un.org/News/dh/infocus/middle_east/Gaza_Flotilla_Panel_Report.pdf

Peretz, Sami, "An Angry Erdogan Stands to Harm Israel-Turkey Economic Ties, *Haaretz*, May 17, 2018. As of May 18, 2018:
https://www.haaretz.com/middle-east-news/turkey/.premium-with-diplomatic-crisis-turkey-israel-trade-ties-may-be-in-trouble-1.6095550

Peuch, Jean-Christophe, "Turkey: Prime Minister's Criticism of Israel Does Not Mark Shift in Policy," *Radio Free Europe*, June 10, 2004.

Pfeffer, Anshel, "Israel Supplies Turkey with Military Equipment for First Time Since Gaza Flotilla," *Haaretz*, February 18, 2013. As of April 12, 2018:
http://www.haaretz.com/israel-news/israel-supplies-turkey-with-military-equipment-for-first-time-since-gaza-flotilla-1.504299

Pileggi, Tamar, "Justice Minister Calls for an Independent Kurdistan," *Times of Israel*, January 20, 2016. As of March 30, 2017:
https://www.timesofisrael.com/shaked-calls-for-an-independent-kurdistan/

"PM Netanyahu Thanks Turkey for Plane to Fight Israel's Wildfires," *Daily Sabah*, November 24, 2016. As of March 30, 2017:
https://www.dailysabah.com/diplomacy/2016/11/24/
pm-netanyahu-thanks-turkey-for-plane-to-fight-israels-wildfires

Porter, Gareth, "The Real Reason for Turkey's Shoot-Down of the Russian Jet," *Middle East Eye*, November 30, 2015. As of March 30, 2017:
http://www.middleeasteye.net/columns/real-turkeys-shoot-down-russian-jet-1615790737

"Profile: Free Gaza Movement," *BBC News*, June 1, 2010. As of March 30, 2017:
http://www.bbc.com/news/10202678

"Putin to Visit Turkey and Egypt amid Anger over Trump's Jerusalem Move," Radio Free Europe, December 8, 2017. As of December 8, 2017:
https://www.rferl.org/a/putin-visit-turkey-egypt-middle-east/28905404.html

Rabi, Uzi, and Chelsi Mueller, "The Gulf Arab States and Israel Since 1967: From 'No Negotiation' to Tacit Cooperation," *British Journal of Middle Eastern Studies*, Vol. 44, No. 4, 2017, pp. 576–592. As of April 17, 2018:
https://doi.org/10.1080/13530194.2017.1360013

Ravid, Barak, "Livni, Turkish FM Hold Reconciliation Talks in Brussels," *Haaretz*, March 6, 2009. As of April 12, 2018:
http://www.haaretz.com/print-edition/news/
livni-turkish-fm-hold-reconciliation-talks-in-brussels-1.271540

———, "Peres: Humiliation of Turkey Envoy Does Not Reflect Israel's Diplomacy," *Haaretz*, January 13, 2010. As of April 12, 2018:
http://www.haaretz.com/news/peres-humiliation-of-turkey-envoy-does-not-reflect-israel-s-diplomacy-1.261381

———, "Netanyahu Calls for Kurdish Independence from Iraq," *Haaretz*, June 30, 2014. As of March 30, 2017:
https://www.haaretz.com/.premium-netanyahu-backs-kurdish-independence-1.5253861

———, "Egypt Asks Israel to Keep Turkey Away from Gaza," *Haaretz*, January 7, 2016. As of March 30, 2017:
https://www.haaretz.com/israel-news/egypt-to-israel-keep-turkey-out-of-gaza-1.5387392

———, "Israel Responds to Erdogan: Temple Mount Statements 'Unfounded and Distorted,'" *Haaretz*, July 25, 2017. As of April 12, 2018:
http://www.haaretz.com/israel-news/1.803407

Raz-Chaimovich, Michal, "Israeli Vacationers Desert Eilat for Cyprus," *Globes*, August 21, 2017. As of August 21, 2017:
http://www.globes.co.il/en/article-israeli-vacationers-desert-eilat-for-cyprus-1001202140

Republic of Turkey, "Turkish Consulate General in Jerusalem," webpage, undated. As of April 12, 2018:
http://jerusalem.cg.mfa.gov.tr/Mission/MissionChiefHistory

Rosenberg, David, "Why Isn't Egypt Joining Israel's Natural Gas Deal Party?" *Haaretz*, February 20, 2018. As of March 16, 2018:
https://www.haaretz.com/israel-news/huge-15-billion-israel-egypt-gas-deal-is-a-mirage-1.5840826

Shargai, Nadav, "Ha'Pe Shel Erdoğan, Ha'Milim Shel Hamas," *Israel Hayom*, December 28, 2017. As of December 28, 2017:
http://www.israelhayom.co.il/article/524425

Stefanini, Sara, "Cyprus Fears Russia Could Wreck Reunification," *Politico*, January 12, 2017. As of March 30, 2017:
http://www.politico.eu/article/cyprus-fears-russia-could-wreck-reunification

"Syria and Turkey—A History of a Complex Relationship," *EU News*, July 28, 2015.

Tagliapietra, Simone, "Is the EastMed Gas Pipeline Just Another EU Pipe Dream?" *Bruegel*, May 10, 2017. As of May 10, 2017:
http://bruegel.org/2017/05/is-the-eastmed-gas-pipeline-just-another-eu-pipe-dream

Tahhan, Zena, "Egypt-Israel Relations 'at Highest Level' in History," *Al Jazeera*, September 20, 2017. As of September 20, 2017:
http://www.aljazeera.com/indepth/features/2016/11/egypt-israel-relations-highest-level-history-161107083926863.html

Tastekin, Fehim, "Turkey, Iran, Iraq in Shaky Alignment Against Iraqi Kurdistan," *Al-Monitor*, September 29, 2017. As of September 29, 2017:
http://www.al-monitor.com/pulse/originals/2017/09/turkey-iran-iraq-alignment-against-iraqi-kurdistan.html#ixzz52LVUulmn

"Turkey-Israel Relations: A Timeline," *Haberler.com*, June 27, 2016. As of March 30, 2017:
https://en.haberler.com/turkey-israel-relations-a-timeline-938803

"Turkish-Israeli Economic, Trade Ties Expected to Soar After Deal," *Hurriyet Daily News*, June 27, 2016. As of March 30, 2017:
http://www.hurriyetdailynews.com/turkish-israeli-economic-trade-ties-expected-to-soar-after-deal.aspx?PageID=238&NID=100945&NewsCatID=345

"Turkey and Israel: Animosity Ends When It Comes to Money," *Deutsche Welle*, December 12, 2017. As of December 12, 2017:
http://www.dw.com/en/turkey-and-israel-animosity-ends-when-it-comes-to-money/a-41766113

"Turkey Rebuilds 9 Mosques in Gaza," *Anadolu Agency*, November 15, 2016. As of March 30, 2017:
http://aa.com.tr/en/middle-east/turkey-rebuilds-9-mosques-in-gaza/685937

"Turkey Sees No Need for Cyprus to Approve Israel Gas Pipeline," *Bloomberg*, April 13, 2017. As of April 13, 2017:
http://www.watertowndailytimes.com/national/turkey-sees-no-need-for-cyprus-to-approve-israel-gas-pipeline-20170413

"Turkish Businesspeople Seek Trade Boost with Israel," *Anadolu Agency*, November 27, 2017. As of January 10, 2018:
http://www.hurriyetdailynews.com/turkish-businesspeople-seek-trade-boost-with-israel-123133

"Turkish FM: No Danger to Israel-Turkey Relations," *Arutz Sheva*, January 7, 2018. As of January 7, 2018:
http://www.israelnationalnews.com/News/Flash.aspx/407779

"Turkish Foreign Ministry Voices Solidarity with TIKA Worker Arrested by Israel," *Hurriyet Daily News*, March 22, 2017. As of March 30, 2017:
http://www.hurriyetdailynews.com/turkish-foreign-ministry-voices-solidarity-with-tika-worker-arrested-by-israel-.aspx?pageID=238&nID=111101&NewsCatID=510

Tzou, Verdi, "Visas Resume Between U.S. and Turkey After Ankara's Promises," *The Cipher Brief*, November 6, 2017. As of November 6, 2017:
https://www.thecipherbrief.com/article/exclusive/middle-east/visas-resume-us-turkey-ankaras-promises

Udasin, Sharon, "Turkish Industrial Leaders Call for Trade Increase with Israel," *Jerusalem Post*, May 16, 2017. As of May 16, 2017:
http://www.jpost.com/Israel-News/Politics-And-Diplomacy/Turkish-industrial-leaders-call-for-trade-increase-with-Israel-490952

Ulutas, Ufuk, "Turkey-Israel: A Fluctuating Alliance," *SETA Policy Brief*, No. 42, January 2010.

University of Haifa and the Hudson Institute, *Report of the Commission on the Eastern Mediterranean*, September 2016. As of March 30, 2017:
https://s3.amazonaws.com/media.hudson.org/files/publications/20160901REPORTOFTHECOMMISSIONONTHEEASTERNMEDITERRANEAN.pdf

Washington Institute for Near East Policy, "Timeline of Turkish-Israeli Relations, 1949–2006," 2006. As of March 30, 2017:
https://www.scribd.com/document/323276049/Turkish-Israel-relationship-Time-line-from-1949-2006

Weiss, Michael, "Turkish TV Depicts IDF as Bloodthirsty," *Tablet Magazine*, October 15, 2009. As of March 30, 2017:
http://www.tabletmag.com/scroll/18437/turkish-tv-depicts-idf-as-bloodthirsty

Williams, Dan, "Israel Tells U.S. Kurdish Independence Is 'Foregone Conclusion,'" Reuters, June 26, 2014. As of March 30, 2017:
https://www.reuters.com/article/us-iraq-crisis-israel-kurds/israel-tells-u-s-kurdish-independence-is-foregone-conclusion-idUSKBN0F11I520140626

Zaman, Amberin, "Erdogan Draws Red Line over US Embassy's Move to Jerusalem," *Al-Monitor*, December 5, 2017. As of December 5, 2017:
http://www.al-monitor.com/pulse/originals/2017/12/erdogan-threates-cut-ties-israel-us-recognize-jerusalem.html#ixzz50vtMWl00

Zeevi, Dror, "Ha'Antishemiyut Ha'Akrait Shel Erdoğan," *Forum for Regional Thinking*, September 3, 2013. As of January 10, 2018:
http://www.regthink.org/articles/האנטישמיות